# Energy Awareness

## *My Guide to Balanced Relationships*

"In Light & Love" Series - Book 3

## Lisa Gornall

This work is solely for personal growth, education, and recreation. It is not a therapeutic activity, such as psychotherapy, counseling, or medical advice, and it should not be treated as a substitute for any professional assistance. In the event of physical or mental distress, please consult with appropriate professionals. The application of protocols and information in this book is the choice of each reader, who assumes full responsibility for his or her understandings, interpretations, and results. The author and the publisher assume no responsibility for the actions or choices of any reader.

# Contents

# Acknowledgments

Thank you to Daniel Franks for a beautiful photograph for this book cover. Relationships are all about balance and you captured it perfectly in this picture. Thank you, Kevin for making a beautiful book cover.

I am grateful for my mom and dad. You are both very intuitive and watching you both as a child helped me become aware of my abilities at a young age. I can see some of your intuitive abilities in me and in my daughters. I love you both! Thank you for everything!

Thank you to everyone in my large family. I love all the energetic experiences that come with being a part of a big family. We have some amazing memories.

I am thankful and grateful for all of my clients and the experiences we have shared together. You make my purpose and passion a reality. A special thank you to Rebecca, Erica, and Bette for supporting my energy work in the beginning and as it continues to go out into the world in even bigger ways.

Thank you to my readers. By reading these books and becoming aware of your energy, you create balance not only in your lives, but in those around you as well. This is how you make a shift in the world. Light conquers the darkness, always. Thank you for spreading the light!

# Foreword

Relationships are an integral part of your life. They shape you just as you shape the people in your relationships. Some of your relationships are amazing and healthy, some are not balanced, other relationships you are indifferent to, and others literally suck the life out of you. All the relationships in your life have a purpose and a reason for being in your life at the exact moment they are. However, how each relationship affects you is completely within your control.

You watch how you spend money, but are you aware of how you spend your energy? What energizes you, what drains you, what helps you make a difference in the world? More specifically, what relationships energize and drain you? Where do you put your energy and what do you get back from these relationships?

In no relationship are you truly a victim without a choice. Before you are born into each life experience you choose your friends, your significant others, your family, your experiences, and even obstacles to help you stay on your path. The people in your life are around you for a reason. Perhaps they are helping you heal past experiences, or maybe they are in your life to help guide you to your next experience. Often, you will not know the reason or purpose someone is in your life immediately. It may takes months, years, or decades to fully know the reason you were involved with each other. Sometimes, you may not appreciate and fully understand an experience with someone for lifetimes.

It is important to remember that everything has a purpose and happens in your life in the exact moment it should. There are no accidents, but there is always free will. You can decide to carry the baggage of past hurts from relationships or you can choose to heal them. You can choose to stay stuck or to be free. You are full of choices in every moment and if you do not like what you are choosing, you can shift directions and get back on the path that is right for you. Relationships shift, change, grow, and disappear as you and the people in your life change. No one is stagnant and exactly the same. The experiences everyone has in their lives gives them opportunities to change paths, live life more purposefully, and to make a difference in the world.

You never know when something may be a last with someone, like a last dinner, a last conversation, or a last time you will see them. Always make your time with people count. The next moment is not guaranteed. You may treat people as if it does not matter how you leave something because you can fix it later. Sometimes, there is no later or next time, and that is when people have regrets. It is time to start paying attention to what you are doing in your relationships and why. All relationships have their ups and downs, but relationships are more fulfilling if you are aware of what you are creating with that person as you are creating it.

## *How to Use This Book*

This is the third book in my "In Light & Love," series. Its purpose is to help you become aware of and understand the energetic exchanges in your relationships that will not only benefit you, but the people you spend your time with as well. This book builds upon the detailed exercises in my first two books and focuses on understanding the energy exchanges in your relationships and how to get back in balance. The exercises in this book are blended into paragraphs as needed to help you in that moment, but please feel free to return to "In Light & Love: My Guide to Balance," for detailed exercises on the energy work basics, or "Energy Balance: My Guide to Transformation," for more detailed exercises to help you through big and life-altering changes.

This book is an important addition to the "In Light & Love," series, because it helps you get to the core of whatever it is time for you to shift in your relationships. When it comes to relationships and patterns, you have to get to the core of what is happening so you can let it go, and then you can reprogram those areas energetically. If you understand what is happening energetically and that everything is happening because you choose for it to happen, it makes it easier to consciously create in your life. The more you do this, the more you elevate your relationships and the more fulfilling they will be for everyone involved.

The chapters are filled with tips and tools to really help you understand what is happening and how to get back in balance. Some of the topics in the book may seem simple, but energy is simple when you understand it. This means that it is easy to incorporate what you read in here into your daily life. Take a moment to look at the chapter titles and see which ones you could use help with now. You can feel free to start there or wherever you feel it will help you the most.

Use this book to empower you, support you, and guide you to make the necessary shifts in your relationships so that they can be balanced. Relationships can be extremely complicated when you do not understand all the energetic pieces that are in play. Most things are not at face value in our society, but they can be more clear if everyone is aware of what they are creating and why. You only have so much time in this life, spend it wisely.

In light & love,

Lisa

# 1 – Your Relationship with Yourself

The relationship you have with yourself is the most important relationship. How you treat yourself is how others treat you. They follow your lead. You set the stage. If you do not think you are worth loving, you will find that the people in your relationships do not love you either. If you feel like you cannot trust anyone, you will notice that your relationships are filled with people you do not trust. Whatever you believe to be true about how relationships are, is what you create in your life. What are the relationships in your life like? Are you happy with them or is it time to change them? What in your life has shaped your current relationships?

Your relationships have many purposes and one of the most important ones is for you to return to a place of love in all of them. No matter what has happened in your life, at your core, you are a being of love. In all your interactions, love is possible. If you find that love is not in a situation or relationship, you have a choice: to either return it to a place of love or to leave it and send it love. In this chapter, learn how self-love, self-worth, your power, patterns, and continually evolving create...you.

## *Self-Love*

You cannot get self-love through other relationships. It is something that has to come from within you and it is within you.

Love is your core energy, but sometimes you may choose to block it, ignore it, or deny it. When this happens no one else can love you enough to make up for you not loving, honoring, and respecting yourself, nor can you buy anything as a substitute. Nothing should alter your self-love because it comes from within, but sometimes you forget all of this.

Can you be alone by yourself or do you always surround yourself with others and noise? Are you afraid of the dialogue in your head? If you are, "Letting Go," in chapter seven is key. It is vital for you to be able to be alone with yourself in silence. Not just in meditation, but for you to be able to sit and just be with yourself and appreciate your life, your being, your experiences, and your journey. You need this time to unplug and reconnect with yourself especially when there is so much craziness happening around you. No one else can do it for you, and it is important for you to just be so you can take care of you.

Self-love is key to creating nurturing and supportive relationships in your life. If you do not value yourself, how will others value you? Self-love is not necessarily just something that forms in this life, although it is heavily influenced in your childhood and from other-life experiences. Regardless of what is preventing you from loving yourself, it is important to let it go and remember that you are a being of love. Love is your natural state, always. Everything else is an illusion.

## You Are Love

You come into this world as a being of love in a bright, white, light and you leave in a bright, white, light. You do this because you are that light and that light flows through you. That light is love and it is what you are made of. Visually, you can see love as a White Light.

If you are having a hard time being alone or loving yourself, remember that you truly are never alone. You are a part of this light, something bigger that is complete love. Let the love into your life, fill your being with it, and let go of any negativity or thoughts telling you that you do not deserve it, or you are not good enough. These thoughts are not true. When you feel yourself starting to sabotage yourself, stop immediately. Freeze the thought, put it on ice, imagine a stop sign stopping it, or whatever works to help you stop it. Then, be grateful for whatever you are truly grateful for in that moment. It has to be true, not what you think you should be grateful for. Let that grateful energy flow from the top of your head, down to your feet, and into the Earth. "I am love. Love is at my core. I spread love into all of my relationships."

Your light shines bright; it is always there for you and it is your self-love. You just have to remember it is there. You are made of this light and all negativity is an illusion that disappears when you remember and live this truth. Self-love is not a choice, rather it is a choice to reject it. This does not help you or those around you. Return to the light, share the light with others, and put the light into all your experiences.

## *Self-Worth*

Your self-worth should not be defined by your relationships, your material objects, or how much money you have or do not have. It is established by connecting with your purpose, your passion, and how you are contributing to the world. You cannot buy self-worth. It comes from within and amplifies when you are aligned with your purpose. If you are not connecting with your self-worth, then it is time for you to look within and ask how you can make a difference in the world. What are you here to do? What can you offer with all of your abilities, talents, and gifts? What are you passionate about? How can you share this with the world? Sometimes, this is connected with your work that pays the bills. Other times, it is not tied to your work, you just bring it with you wherever you go.

No one can give you your self-worth or take it away. This is something else that has to come from within you. If you feel like it is missing, you may find yourself trying to keep busy with other things at work and in your relationships. Busy work will not make you feel fulfilled. It will leave you feeling empty because it is not purposeful.

At your core, you know that you are here for a purpose. You are guided by your passion and you bring to the table so many things to help make a difference in the world. If you have been distracted, you will know it is time to shift gears and reconnect with this when you feel empty, miserable, and unfulfilled. It is easy to get distracted from your purpose, but your spirit will grow restless and you will feel an intense need to reconnect with it and get back on track. You are here for a purpose and no one can take that away from you or do it for you. This is something only you can do and you have the tools to do it. You were born with them. Appreciate your unique value!

## *Your Power*

Power is an energy exchange in all relationships and, ideally it is an equal one. Whether exerting your will on someone else, someone exerting their will on you, or in an equal energy exchange, it is important to be aware of what you are doing with your power. What you are doing and not doing with your power directly affects your energy and your relationships.

### Balance Your Power in Relationships

Imagine that all the relationships you encounter are happening on a spider web so that you can see how what happens in one area affects the whole web. If you give away your power, you let your web break free from where it is anchored. The more it breaks free, the weaker and less empowered you feel until you are ready to break free from that relationship. When you exert your power on someone else, energetically it is as though you are pinning them onto your web which will weigh it down. Eventually this will cause a hole in the web and in your relationship as well. If the relationship is balanced energetically, the web stays intact as does the relationship, your self-esteem, and your power.

Think about the relationships in your life and notice what type of web each one has. At some point everyone realizes that they are ready for balanced and equal relationships. Anything else takes too much energy and ends up causing too many problems. What are some things you can do in your relationships to make the web balanced and equal for everyone involved? Is this something you are ready to fix? If not, you will when the time is right for you. In the meantime, watch the web and your energy and see how they correlate with each other. In what relationships do you give away your power, over-power others, and which ones are balanced? By creating equal relationships, you help everyone involved. What does this mean to you and how does it relate to your patterns?

## *Your Patterns*

Take time to notice who you spend the most time with at work, at home, and when you are with family. Do these people support you or do they bring you down? What is your role in the relationship? Do you still want this to be your role?

Relationships are complicated because there are so many more things happening than meets the eye. Many people do not want to be like their parents and they end up taking on their beliefs, behaviors, and patterns without realizing they did. Everything that you are doing in your relationships, you are choosing to do. The good news is that if you do not like something, you can change it. If you do like how things are, you can keep doing what you are doing.

Become aware of any patterns that you have created and see if these patterns are working for you, if you are avoiding them, or if you want to change them but keep recreating them. The patterns in your life are fine until they no longer support you and they are causing you problems. Once they are causing problems, it becomes time to change them. Begin by noticing what your behavior is in your relationships. Are you a helper, a giver, a taker, a user, a victim, a _____? How does this affect your relationships?

Now ask yourself if your relationships are fulfilling? Do they make you happy or do they make you miserable? How do you feel after spending time with the different people in your life? Is there anything you would like to change or is everything perfect?

Do you notice the same patterns in your relationships or are there patterns in certain relationships? For example, do you continue to have the same problems with the people you work with? Do you notice that all your friends treat you the same way, whether this is a way you would like to be treated or not? Perhaps there is a problem with just one or two friends? How does your significant other treat you? How are your interactions with your family? Do you notice any of the patterns that you have with your family carrying out in other relationships?

By honestly answering all of these questions, you can start to notice what your relationship patterns are, and then pay attention to what is happening when you are with others. If you love all of your relationships and everything is great, then you are probably happy with your patterns. Chances are you have some relationships that you do not like and would like to change. Once you are aware of what it is that you would like to have in your relationships, you can start to make it happen. Some people may leave and others may change and stay.

## Changing Relationship Patterns

It is time to start being aware of what you are doing in your relationships. Notice how you feel when you are doing your patterns with the people around you and what you can start doing differently. Usually, something forces you to change your patterns and that is not the easiest road. The easiest thing is for you to start paying attention to what you are doing and why, how you feel during these interactions, and change these patterns yourself.

You change them by first becoming aware of them. Then, notice when those old patterns are happening and decide not to do what you have always done, do something instead that feels different but right in that moment, and catch yourself if you start to slip back into the old pattern again. For example, if you always give your power over to someone else and you are ready to change this pattern, begin by catching yourself before you hand over your power or the moment you realize you have handed it over. Regain you power back immediately by no longer engaging in the power exchange. In this example, you would start to pay attention to how it feels to pull your energy back and focus on feeling empowered. Then check in and see if there is anything else you should say or do to return balance to this relationship. Perhaps this relationship can use some boundaries or time apart.

It is also important to become aware of any patterns that feel old and familiar because they have been happening across many lifetimes as well. Just because something has been happening for decades or across lifetimes does not mean that is right for you anymore. An example of this pattern is something that you did as a young child. It is not something that anyone else in your family does, but you notice that you have been doing it for as long as you can remember and you do not know why. This is a pattern you have brought in from another life and it is probably ready to be changed. The moment you become aware of a pattern that does not make you feel good, you will notice you want to change it and the time is now.

## *You Are Continually Evolving*

You are not a stagnant being and neither are the people in your relationships. Events happen in your life and they change your views, beliefs, expectations, and perceptions. The person you were as a child shifts as you get older and gain more experiences. You never stop changing and evolving because things are never stagnant.

The goal is for your experiences to help you do what you are here to do so you can experience what you are here to experience. When one experience is complete, you move on to another one. Think about all the changes the people in your life have gone through individually and all the things they have watched you go through. Big life events like graduation, marriage, children, death, divorce, separation, moving, and career changes help you grow as a person. These events give you knowledge, experiences, and perceptions that you did not have before them and you shift and change because of them. As you shift and change, you may notice that your relationships do as well.

## Relationships Shift

You will find that relationships are easier when you are on the same page and going in the same direction. The people in your life may shift with you but, sometimes they cannot or will not. It is not your job to make the other people change, follow you, or be with you. Your job is for you to shift and change with the path you are on. If the people in your life come with you, that is great. If they do not come with you, your paths may be shifting or something may be going on in their life preventing them from being in yours. People are constantly coming into your life, just as people may be leaving. Everything has a time and a purpose.

There are some relationships that appear to stop evolving and this causes problems. Sometimes, people get stuck. They hold onto the baggage of their experiences and sometimes they become angry and bitter. Other times, they may decide to just give up and they appear to have no purpose, direction, or motivation. Sometimes, something happens in a relationship and the other person cannot forgive it or let it go. Many things can happen in a relationship that can bring it to an end. Remember, not all relationships are meant to last a lifetime. If a relationship becomes something you no longer care to participate in, it is time for a change.

Your job is to grow and to support the people in your life in their growing. Remind yourself and them that you are not stagnant. Things happen for a purpose, sometimes you know the purpose and sometimes you will not. What you do know is that your life is full of change, your relationships are full of change, and change is all around you. Embrace it the best you can and know that you are never alone because true happiness, love, and peace come from within. Your relationships are just an extension of what you are feeling from within. The inner reflects the outer, always.

# 2 – Energetically Understanding Your Relationships

Every relationship in your life has a purpose. Something bigger is happening. Sometimes, things are so crazy and out of control you cannot imagine that you ever picked these people to be in your life or that they wanted you to be in theirs. However, that is how it all begins. You and them, in a place of love, before you enter your physical bodies.

Your parents, grandparents, siblings, cousins, friends, co-workers, significant others, and even random strangers all agree to be in your life with you. You picked your family to be yours way before you were even a fetus, possibly even lifetimes ago. You are together because you have things to heal together, support each other with, or to create together. Even in relationships that are difficult, you are purposely together. Everything happens for a reason. The people in your life are here because you chose for them to be. It really is that simple.

Think for a minute about the people in your life, your relationships with them, and how you feel about them. Know that every single one of those relationships have a purpose, not one of them is random. Whether they are good or bad, you have control over the relationships in your life in how you nurture them. In this chapter you will learn how karma, other-life experiences, and mentalities affect relationships.

## *Karma in Your Relationships*

What goes around really does come around instantly in this moment and across lifetimes as well. Karma can take anywhere from one, multiple, or hundreds of lifetimes to heal. It depends on the energy exchange that has to be healed.

Karma is not something only you control. Once you do something to someone else, they also get to choose how to respond to the event and when it will ultimately be healed. The best practice is to do to others as you would like done to you. This sounds easy until someone makes you mad, cuts you off on the freeway, or purposely hurts you. These are important, tell-tale moments. They tell you if you are out of balance based upon how you respond, either from a place of love when you are in balance or from a place not of love if you are out of balance.

Remember that your core is a being of love and light, anything else is an illusion. Negativity is darkness and is not real. Think about when you turn a light on how the darkness disappears so you can see clearly. The same is true energetically and light conquers darkness every time. Yet, as you experience the energy exchanges in your life, you may find that it is easier for you to be angry or upset when someone hurts you, because this is a pattern you have had for decades in your life or for many lifetimes.

Stop letting your light become hidden by the darkness over experiences that at the end of your life will not matter. Do not let them shatter or fragment your energy. Stay in a place of love no matter what is happening around you. You will immediately notice an energetic shift in the events unfolding and the karma that you are receiving the more you act from a place of love.

## Understanding Karma

You will experience the energy you give to someone else the moment you give them that energy, regardless if it is positive or negative. In that moment, that energy exchange ripples across your existence instantly as an energetic flash.

Sometimes, karma is healed right away and these are usually things you have already learned and are ready to let go of and heal. Other times, you have to go through multiple lives having the same experience and patterns to finally distance yourself and be able to make peace with it to heal it in that original life. There is no way to manipulate the karma in your life. You do control how you treat people in every moment which directly affects your karma so, focus on returning to a place of love in every situation; that is your true state of being.

### *We Are All One*

Karma weaves into the present moment and directly into all of your life experiences, energetically connecting them all at once. This is why you can heal things in this life and feel a shift in other-life experiences with that person as well. Karma is actually very complicated and yet simple at the same time. What you do to others you do to yourself every single time, because at our core we are all connected. We are all one. What you do to one, you do to all. You are a part of the all and that is why it affects you. You can visualize the all as a big, brilliant ball of White Light. You are a part of that light and when you join it you are not separate; you become one with the light. You blend in with the White Light and feel peace, love, and happiness.

Energetically, you already know what it feels like to be one with everyone else, just close your eyes and imagine being a part of the ball of White Light. Then imagine coming back to your body. You are physically separated from the ball in this life via your ego, but you are still a part of the White Light because your core is the White Light. Always! Remember this, especially when you get mad or you want to hurt someone, just return back to the ball of light. In this energetic place you will be reminded that we are all one, and whatever is happening in this moment that is not of love has no place in the ball of light. Not now, not ever.

### *Karma is Instant*

Remember that everything you do to others will come back to you instantly. You will feel it the moment it happens. For example, if you yelled at someone, you will feel angry, and if you were kind to someone, you will feel happy. Karma is not something that you directly control, because when you do something to someone else they also have an investment in the energy exchange. You cannot do something to hurt someone and then try to plot how to fix it so you do not receive that negative energy back at you. The moment you do an act, the energy exchange has already happened. It may not be fixed in this life, but it will eventually be resolved in another life. Just as karma from other lives will come to you in this life to heal and the moment it heals here, it heals in the original life it happened in as well. Everything is an energy exchange, everything is connected, and we are all one.

## *The Role of Your Ego*

Your ego is here to help you separate from the all and to help you be here on this planet so you can have the individual experiences and healings you are here to have. The problem is that everyone is straying far from the light and remembering we are all one, to believing that the darkness is more powerful. This is an illusion. Remember, just turn on the energetic light!

Now more than ever, it is important to remember your truth that you are love, peace, and happiness and that negativity and darkness are truly illusions. Your ego does not want to disappear into the White Light; it wants control, power, and separation. You have to find a medium between being physically separate and remembering that we are all one to help balance your being. You are not separate, we are all connected.

## Healing the Past

You store all your past hurts, pains, and frustrations not only from this life but from others as well. Typically, you store them in the same places across lives, almost like a bank of past hurts to not do again. Unfortunately, when you hold onto things across lives, they appear in other lives continually so they can be healed. When do you deal with them? Usually, only when you are forced to deal with them. Typically, they come out in forms of illness or a huge explosion of anger. Once you start healing, you will find more layers that are ready to be released.

Let go of your anger, frustration, resentment, and sadness. Not forgiving someone for what they did holds you back. It puts a huge weight on your energy like a butterfly trying to fly with a rock. Chances are that you too, have done things to them in other lives and whatever happened was supposed to happen because it did. Over-analyzing and rehashing the situation does not change anything. In fact, it keeps building that negative energy. If something is showing up repeatedly in your life, it is usually because it is time to let it go. By letting it go in this life, you will help free yourself of it in other lives as well. There are many layers from all the lives you live. Most likely you will not let go of everything in one lifetime because there are so many layers, but you can continually lessen the load as things come up.

## Karma Is Not Punishment

Yes, people suffer and get hurt. That happens because at some level, that was the experience they chose to have at that time for a specific purpose. Most often it is to shift them and change ongoing patterns in their life. Perhaps karma is happening so they can let something go and return to love. It is not that you like to be hurt to learn a lesson, but sometimes you ignore all the gentle urges to make a shift when a shift has to happen. You get comfortable with things as they are and sometimes change seems scary. Each little urge to shift that you ignore gets bigger and bigger, until something happens drastically in your life to force you to change.

Karma is not at all about punishment rather it is all about healing. Karma shows up most often in relationships or situations that are ready to be healed. Sometimes, you may find new or old acquaintances that will appear at the perfect time to actually help you through something difficult in your life to make it easier for you.

## Becoming Whole Again

In the end, we are all one. We are all love. Everything that happens to you is supposed to happen or it would not happen. You agreed to it before you incarnated into your body, or you are choosing it now, so you can do what you are here to do. There are no accidents. There are no mistakes. Everything has a purpose and that purpose is to always return to a place of love. In a place of love, you are whole again and you stop being fragmented.

You are not meant to be pieces of love or fragmented, you are meant to be whole. You are a beam of love that visually is a part of the ball of White Light. Where you think your love ends, another begins and blends into the end. There is no you and me, just we. We are all one. When you get angry or mad at someone notice how you feel. Where do you feel it and how do you feel? How can you let it go and flow again from a place of love?

Fill yourself with love, light, and peace. This is your true state. Ask yourself what your connection is with this person, what is it time to heal, and how can you heal it? By understanding what this connection is and why it is happening you can start to free yourself and all those around you. There are exercises in chapter seven to help you with this. The lighter you feel energetically, the happier you are. This will attract more happiness to you and more relationships that are balanced and supportive.

## Forgiveness

Forgiveness is just as important for you as it is for the person you are forgiving, because you keep that negative energy tied to both of you. When you forgive someone, you instantly release yourself and them from all the energetic baggage you bind yourselves together with. This means that the moment you truly forgive someone, you are free. This also frees them and instantly you can energetically both shift your energy into healing other things. Being stuck does not help you; it just holds you in limbo. It is important for you to free your energy. You do not forget what you learned, but you will remember without the baggage.

There are many ways to practice forgiveness with yourself and others. The first step is to be aware of where you are holding this energy in your body. Then notice how it makes you feel. What did you learn from this experience? Are you ready to let it go now? Once you are ready to let the energy go it is time to free your energy. There are exercises to help you let this go in chapter seven. At some point, it gets harder to hold onto the baggage, than to let it go and be free. This is when you know you are ready to forgive. Forgiveness sets you free of all the negative energy you are holding onto and it returns you to the light where you belong, whole and free.

## *Forgiving Yourself*

One of the most important people for you to forgive is yourself. You are always the hardest on yourself. Holding your energy prisoner does not change what happened, it does not make you feel better, and it does not hold you accountable for what you did or how you were involved. Rather, it is more of a means to keep you stuck, trapped, unaccountable, and miserable. Free yourself!

You become accountable and free when you own what you did, why you did it, and you learn from the whole experience so you do not do it again. Basically, you get to the core of why you did what you did, if you feel awful for doing it then feel awful, let it all go, and learn from this experience. This is something you do by yourself without involving the other person. They have their own baggage from the situation. You must first clear yourself, then you can apologize, but only if it will help the other person with their healing. If it will only help you, then do not apologize because you will make things worse for them again.

Whenever you hurt someone, at some level it is intentional, and they are typically not interested in your healing or apologies. The moment you hurt someone else their journey is about them healing when they are ready. What you focus on is taking responsibility by truly owning why you did something, how you feel about it, and freeing your energy. You must take full responsibility for your actions and not blame anyone else, or you cannot move on. Period.

You cannot make someone forgive you, but you can forgive yourself if you have done something that has hurt someone else. Learn from your mistakes and do not keep repeating them. Remember, the first step is for you to be accountable and stop hiding behind feeling guilty. You have to own up to what you did and any pain you have caused to move forward, it is the only way. The other person will forgive you when they are ready and that may happen in this life or it may happen in another. You do not control when, they do. In the meantime, you can forgive yourself and learn from the whole experience by not doing it again to anyone else.

## Be Purposeful

One of the most important things for you to do in every moment is to be purposeful with your energy. The thoughts you think create your reality, often instantly. Imagine that everything you think, say, and do bounces right off of you, onto a mirror, and ricochets right back to you. Maybe you do intend to send yourself negative energy, but chances are you do not. If you are purposeful and aware of what you are doing, you can stop a lot of the pain, anger, and frustration you send out from coming back to you by not sending it out in the first place.

Imagine that you just got cut off by a driver who is being rude to you. What do you do with your energy? You probably do not send them love and light even though that is exactly what you should send them. Chances are in that moment you send them anger, frustration, and get all worked up. Sometimes, you get so worked up that you go home and have to tell someone about that experience. Now the driver, perhaps they are rushing to someone they love in a medical emergency. They are not even aware of what you are sending to them in that moment. You however, are still angry hours later. Why? The moment you got mad, angry, and frustrated at them, that reflected right back to you and you received that energy. We all feel the energy around us. You know what it feels like to be with someone who is happy versus angry. You can feel it and that is why it is so important to be purposeful with the energy you give to others.

Now imagine yourself happily doing something for someone that you love and appreciate. Think about how happy that makes you feel as the joy literally pours off of you to the other person. This is a happy energy exchange and is the same karmic energy of, what you do to others will bounce right back to you. It is just a happy one instead of an angry one. The more love you give to others, the more love is returned to you. It is a very simple equation and not one that you can fake or manipulate. Your true intentions bounce back to you in every moment.

Most likely, you have relationships in your life that you are not happy with, or ones that ended years ago and you are still holding onto. Any anger you continue to throw at someone else for any wrongs always hurts you more than them. Remember the example about the driver? You are not hurting the other person more than you are hurting yourself.

Karma is happening in all of your relationships and the best way to break some of your harmful relationship patterns is to be aware of what you are doing to others and why. Always ask yourself how you would feel if someone was doing to you what you are doing to others. On the flip side, if you do not like what someone is doing to you, then change that pattern. Sometimes, those patterns are from lifetimes ago and it is time for you to change them now.

## *Other-Life Experiences*

Everyone comes into the world heavily influenced from other-life experiences and the karma from those experiences. This happens because something that you cannot heal with someone in another life because it is too difficult at that time, energetically carries over into multiple lives together until you can heal it. For example, a significant other in one experience that died young will pull out something different in you compared to a person that imprisoned you. A special teacher or close sibling will stir up different feelings when you meet them compared to a person that broke your trust. Energetically, you carry your baggage throughout your lifetimes until you are ready to heal it.

All the people in your life you have had other-life experiences with, and they are heavily influenced by karma. You may notice certain things are stirred up within you when you are with certain people. Some of that past baggage is brought into this life to help you get closer to healing it. Other times, you will find it is time to set it free for both of you. For example, you may spend lifetimes working on forgiving someone for hurting you emotionally or physically. They will appear in multiple lives with you dealing with that past karma in ways that you have power over them and you may even become the abuser. You will continue to have different situations together until you are able to forgive them, and in doing so you heal the energy. Instantly, you both shift and become free from that baggage.

Other-lives heavily influence your day-to-day encounters. Perhaps, you are drawn to someone like a magnet and you immediately bond. Sometimes, you are indifferent to someone who is drawn to you. Of course, there are also the people you immediately dislike and want to run away from. All of these are examples of other-life experiences surfacing to help you with something. You will not often understand the karmic or other-life undertones in your relationships the moment they are happening, but they heavily influence you, so it is good to be aware of them.

## Instant Connection

Being drawn to someone feels good instantly in the moment you meet them. The connection energetically feels as if you are magnetically being pulled together. Sometimes, that relationship lasts for decades, sometimes it is only meant for a short time.

Whenever you have that connection with someone, that positive feeling is happening for a reason, so pay attention. Perhaps, they are there to help you learn to love and be better in a relationship, or they may be helping you with an experience or change you are having a hard time with. It simply depends on what you two decide should happen before you were born, and then what paths you take in this life because of your free will. In these relationships, you have both signed up to literally help each other through something intense in your lives. You can help each other in special ways others cannot because of this connection.

## Soul Mates

Soul mates are instant connections you feel when you meet someone. They feel familiar to you because they are. When you meet them you feel an instant, familiar, I know you feeling. Sometimes, your soul mates are people you have had intimate, significant other relationships with before, and sometimes you have had special family relationships or friendships. Sometimes, these people were siblings, best friends, teachers, parents, grandparents, or people that you have done important things with.

Soul mates are usually good friends. Think about how you energetically feel when you think of a soul mate and then the people in your life that are your soul mates. You did not come on this journey alone. You have teamed up with different soul mates to support you and for you to support them in different areas. Sometimes, they help you with things that you have dealt with before. Other times, they come in to help you with something that is intense, but because of your past love and trust, they are able to help you through it.

## Meeting "The One"

Another example of an immediate, instant connection is when people talk about meeting the love of their life or, "The One." What happens when you meet this person is that you know immediately and instantly in a second that you are meant to be with them. You will have an intense pull and connection with them that you have probably not felt before. You are intoxicatingly drawn to them so much so, that you cannot imagine your life without them.

It is a conscious choice to be with "The One," or to settle for anyone else. Whatever you choose tells you what you are working on. In our society, as romanticized as finding "The One," is and knowing when you meet them, some people may still run the other direction at first, because the connection is so intense it scares them. Once that passes, energetically you feel a pull to step up to the plate and engage in a way you have not before with another partner. All the hiding, games, being distant, and anything else you have done to push away your partners before is not possible when you know, because you do not want to end the relationship for good. You are energetically pulled together.

Being in a relationship with "The One," is usually longer lasting than being in a relationship with someone you grow to love or even a romantic relationship with a soul mate. Relationships have their ups and downs and it is easier to stay in a relationship during the roller coaster if you have an intense, magnetic connection with your partner. Otherwise, it is easier to walk away and start over with someone else because that special connection is not there. You will feel you can have a better relationship with anyone else when things are rough if you are not in a relationship with "The One."

Our society romanticizes about this connection more than any other relationship. It feels like a drug because it is such a pure and intense experience. At the same time, this connection forces us to shed whatever keeps us from connecting. If you are able to, you will find that you can work through things with this person that you cannot with anyone else. This is a powerful connection and not one that everyone will allow in their lifetime. It is a choice.

### Timing is not Right in a Relationship

Sometimes, it seems that the timing is not right but remember there are no accidents. Everything happens when and as it should. This means you are connecting to heal or help each other with something. Typically, this happens when this person has been "The One," for you in another life and the connection is familiar, but it is not magnetic. You have a connection in this life, but it feels more like a soul mate because there is no intense, magnetic pull. Whatever they trigger in you is something they are temporarily appearing to help you remember and you have made this agreement together before being born in this life.

If the person gets away, they are not "The One," for you in this life. Their purpose is to get your attention and most likely to help you refocus or redirect something in your life. Sometimes, you only have to feel a connection with someone to help you through something and that is all you are together for in this life. Other times, the intimacy of the relationship may scare you and you do not want to give your heart to someone, so you do not engage. Many people choose to go their whole life without meeting or engaging in a relationship with "The One." Usually, if this happens, that person is seriously avoiding it at all costs, and this does happen. However, it is possible for everyone to be in a relationship with "The One." It is all about what type of relationships you choose to accept and have in your life.

## Indifferent Connections

Indifferent connections form when you first meet someone and you are not drawn like a magnet, nor are you repelled from them. These are often the connections in which you grow to like or love someone. Sometimes, they are colleagues that may become friends. They may be people you become attracted to and they become a significant other for a period of time. They may be a part of your life for a few months to many years. Like all relationships, it just depends on what you are working on energetically together.

These are not typically relationships that will last a lifetime, rather for a period of time. Most of the relationships that are in your life are this type of connection. They are there for a purpose, for a specific period of time, and not necessarily a lifetime. For example, a colleague that grows to become your friend will most likely not turn into a life-long friend. Your connection with them is to help each other through something in this life like changes in the work environment, and sometimes they help through relationship or life changes. Often, they are in your life for a short period of time and when you are not around them daily or often, the connection disappears. They are around for a few weeks, months, or a few years and they are easily replaced with someone else when the relationship drifts away. There is nothing that pulls you or connects you together, so these relationships easily fade since they are not an instant connection.

## Romantic Relationships

Indifferent connections can turn into romantic relationships. Some examples are when you start dating a friend, you settle for someone and decide to stay in the relationship, or you feel a purely physical attraction to someone. Sometimes, people even get married just because they did not think anyone else would want them, they were together so long they felt they had to, or something happens and they think they should. All of these relationships are very different energy connections than "The One," connection.

When things get hard or difficult as they do in all relationships, it can be harder to make these relationships work because there is no special, intense, magnetic pull to keep you there. Nothing makes this relationship essential to keep you in it. You feel like you can move to where the grass looks greener because there is nothing special energetically in this relationship pulling you together to help you through the ups and downs of life, so the grass does feel and look greener with other people.

It is not uncommon for these relationships to end and to have multiple versions of them in a lifetime. If you are in this type of relationship and you are not aware of who you are connecting with and why, you will probably continue to create the same type of relationships. Do not settle, because this does not help you or the other person. If you are open to being in a relationship with someone that you have an instant connection with, you will not be interested in romantic relationships with indifferent connections anymore. Once you have more, you will be ready for more from your relationships.

## Instant Disconnections

Just as being drawn to someone is instantly noticeable, wanting to run away when you meet someone you instantly dislike is an immediate red flag. You may have examples where you have ignored this instant disconnection and immediate dislike only to regret it later by saying something like: "I had a bad feeling about them. I did not trust myself. I knew they were not good for me."

Always trust your intuition with people, especially when you have a bad feeling. You have a bad feeling for a reason. Each situation is different, but the people you hold most dear to you in your life are not from instant disconnections. Think about your experiences with this connection type and how they have often ended, that is if you even gave them a chance to begin.

Just like the other relationship connections, something bigger is going on in this situation. You do not have to be their best friend or invite them to your house, but look deeper and find out what is happening here. This interaction leaves you uncomfortable and that tells you that they are triggering something in you that is unfinished. They are appearing to help you make peace with whatever that is. Almost always, you are picking up on karma with this person from another life and maybe you can be distant enough from that other experience to heal it in this life. Ideally, that is the goal, to let stuff go when it has no place in this moment.

## *"Me Mentality" versus "We Mentality"*

There are two mentality types, the "Me Mentality," and the "We Mentality." Understanding where you and the other person are focused is helpful in understanding the dynamics in a relationship. People are where they are because that is where they choose to be. The purpose of this section is not to judge yourself or someone else, rather to understand where everyone is coming from.

## "Me Mentality"

In the "Me Mentality," the person is focused on me and what is best for me. They are ego driven and focused on their own needs and wants, no matter how this affects others and the whole. The ego does separate us from each other, and its role is to make us think that we are separate even though we really are all connected and we are a part of the whole. This allows you to have the experiences that you are here to have, however the goal is to have your experiences and to remember that we are all one and connected.

From this place, people do not worry about how their actions affect anyone else, rather they focus on what will best serve them in that moment. Often, when you are around someone in this mentality, you may find that they pull you down or that they bother you because they are always messing around. People in this category are often described by others as victims, self-serving, drama lovers, or they are energy drainers. If you decide to take care of someone that hurt you with an eye for an eye approach, this is the "Me Mentality." Also, if your actions are secretive or if you intentionally are doing something to hurt someone, this also comes from this mentality.

If you are in a relationship that is abusive, unequal, unfulfilling, painful, or one that you are in because you do not know how to leave, you have experienced what the "Me Mentality," feels like. It is toxic in relationships when the focus becomes unbalanced and completely focused on the needs of one person above everyone else. If you have been in a "Me Mentality," relationship and decide to take care of yourself by doing something to support yourself like going on vacation, taking time to be, spending time in nature, doing an activity that you love, finding support to help you, or leaving the relationship because you have tried and there is nothing else you can do, that does not put you in the "Me Mentality."

Simply taking care of yourself does not put you into the "Me Mentality," because this is necessary to keep you from burning out. However, if you do something intentionally to hurt someone else, if you become a victim and stay there, or you get in a place that you only care about your needs and wants, that does shift you into the "Me Mentality," because that hurts the people around you. Basically, the me focuses on me instead of we.

## "We Mentality"

On the flip side, people in the "We Mentality," focus mostly on big picture and how it affects everyone. They realize that what they do not only affects them and comes back to them, but ripples out to those around them. People in this category are often helpers or healers.

The goal is for everyone to find their way back to this mentality a majority of the time. Everyone can and should find a way to return back to the "We Mentality." Energetically, everyone is feeling the pulls, accidents, injuries, and shifts in their lives to make this happen. As a society, we can no longer function from a place of me, because it is hurting too many things.

Being part of the "We Mentality," does not mean that you completely give up your sense of self, your dreams, and your purpose. Rather, you use these things that are special about you to make a difference, live your purpose, and think big picture. This will in turn help others, because what you do directly affects everyone else.

During big changes, it is a time for you to look within and see what has to shift to help you move forward. Society may say that this is a me time, but it can still be done in a we way. As you make the changes in your life, ask how this change will help you make a difference in the world. How can you use your passion and purpose to raise your energy level and those around you as well?

## How Mentality Affects Relationships

Depending on which mentality you relate to determines on how well you deal with the "Me Mentality." If you have two "Me Mentalities," in a relationship, it is usually not long-lasting simply because they cannot focus on or meet the other person's needs, so it does not work. Plus, there is usually a lot of drama. See more on drama in chapter four.

When there is a "We Mentality," in a relationship with a "Me Mentality," the "We Mentality," usually gets frustrated and leaves the relationship. This is because the relationship is not equal. The "We Mentality," may try to help or fix the "Me Mentality," but eventually it becomes too draining for the "We Mentality," when they cannot help the person make the changes. Remember, you cannot make someone else change. You only have the power to change yourself.

Typically, the most successful and happy relationships are with people who are both in the "We Mentality," because they are focused on others and raising their energy together. After all, that is the purpose of coming together, to raise each other up and be equals. In a "Me Mentality," there are no equals, rather it is one-sided.

# 3 – Communicating Effectively

Communication in every relationship is key. A conversation can prevent a fight or start one. Are your words conveying your message in the way you intend, or is your message being misunderstood? What feelings are driving your communication? Are you coming from a place of anger, fear, stress, or sadness? If you are, how differently would your communication be received if it came from a place of peace and love? Is your intent to make a change or to keep doing the same pattern? This is key!

Almost always, the biggest complaint in relationships deals with the way something is or is not being communicated. Whether the problem is not understanding what they meant, feeling like you are not being heard, lying, or your message not getting across, what you say, how you say it, when you say it, and what you do not say has a great impact on all of your relationships.

## *Understanding Your Communications*

One of the biggest problems in relationships is communication. Not being heard, misunderstandings, not telling the truth, and fighting with no resolution are just some problems. It all boils down to communicating. Is what you are actually saying being understood correctly? Is there another way to say something in a way that it will be better heard? What are you saying non-verbally with your actions, your facial expressions, and your energy?

Pay attention to your energy and theirs. If you are not in a good place, it does not matter what you say, it will most likely not come across well because the other person will be reading your energy or the vibes you are giving them. If you are saying one thing and contradicting it with your energy, that will send a mixed signal. For example, if you say that you are okay with something they are doing, but you seem angry and agitated, this is confusing. It sends a mixed signal and it muddies the communication because they do not know what you actually mean. Sometimes, it is best to wait for important communications to happen until you are in a good or more balanced place, that way it will be more effective.

A good practice, is to pay attention to how you deliver a message to make sure it is received clearly. You can always say, "I feel _____." This will clearly let people know how you feel and they cannot disagree with how you feel because they are not you. If they do disagree with how you feel, then something else is happening. Why are they not listening and trying to fix something that is bothering you? Perhaps the relationship needs distance, help from a third party, or maybe it is complete.

Make sure that you are communicating with the people in your life. If you are not communicating with them, they often do not know what is going on. As you can imagine, this causes many problems too. Communication is important to create a successful relationship. Remember, there are some mind readers out there, but they are not the majority of the people you are dealing with. You have to speak and listen in ways that help the relationship move forward.

No matter what you do, make sure you are talking clearly with the people in your life, this helps them know what to do and what not to do. It also helps squash an irritation before it becomes a huge problem.

## Listen and Understand

Listen to the words people are saying to you. They say what they truly mean over and over again. If you are not listening, that is not their fault. Their words are their truth, beliefs, and expectations. That does not mean you have to agree, but to have a common ground, you have to understand where they are coming from and they should understand where you are coming from. If you do not understand what they are trying to tell you, then nicely let them know that you do not understand and specifically what you are having a hard time grasping. If there continues to be confusion after many attempts then clearly, something has to change.

Words are used to communicate so many feelings. If someone is communicating their feelings to you, especially about your relationship together, listen. When the people in your life are aware of a problem and they want to fix it, they will tell you about it. They will also tell you the things they like and do not like. If the two of you can listen and try to incorporate expectations into the relationship, things will be much smoother for both of you.

## Pay Attention

One of the biggest problems in communication is that someone is not always paying attention. Perhaps they get a text, a social media alert, emails, are watching television, are on the computer, listening to music, etc. This happens in a lot of your daily interactions. Sometimes, you do it to others and other times they do it to you.

While it seems okay to multi-task while you are listening to someone, you will find that you do not hear everything they said to you. You may hear a part of it or none of it and just grunt or agree to show you heard them. Chances are if someone asks you to repeat back everything they said, you will not be able to. You may remember the end part, but not the whole point. You can see how this can cause communication problems. Most people do not like to repeat themselves.

If someone is taking the time to speak to you and they are in front of you that should be your priority. Everything else can wait until this communication is complete. You feel that if you get a text, an email, a phone call, or an alert that your priority should shift to this because it just happened. The reality is that if you keep ignoring the people in front of you, they will eventually stop trying to talk to you because they are done not being heard, or you will end up in a lot of miscommunication fights.

Put your phone and other electronic gadgets away when you are meeting someone to spend time together. Otherwise, you could have stayed home and you would not be ignoring or offending anyone. Notice that when you put your phone away and you do not look at it, others will not either, even if their hand is permanently attached to technology. If you are not on yours and they are, it will make them uncomfortable and question being plugged in. You show others how to treat you by what you do to them.

## Speak Clearly

Say what you mean to say because when you do not, you create drama in your life. If you want someone to help you with something, ask them to help you. Do not hint around it. That is confusing and sometimes people do not understand or get your hints. If you are confused by what someone is saying for you to do, do not try to read between the lines. Ask for clarity.

For example, do not tell someone not to get you a gift for something and then be mad when they do not. This happens all the time! From the perspective of the other person, they were simply following your instructions and they are completely bewildered when you are upset. If you want someone to get you a gift, do not tell them not to. When you tell people the opposite of what you really mean all the time, they have no idea what to do and this will cause problems. In the end, it is very confusing and difficult to be in a relationship with someone when you do not understand what they want because they do not say what they truly mean.

Likewise, sometimes you think people can read your mind and they should just know something. Even if they can read your mind or you know them very well, it is important for everyone to be able to say what is important for them to say and for them to be heard. Remember, most people are not mind readers. Instead, speak clearly and in a way that people can relate to what you are saying and understand it.

Also, make sure you are communicating out loud to someone. Sometimes, you think the conversation in your mind, but you do not actually say the words to them. This may happen when you are busy and growing angrier as someone watches you do something and you are thinking, "Help me!" Perhaps, you may just be thinking in your head and growing angrier thinking, "This is taking too long." However, the other person just sees you getting angry and they do not know why because you are not telling them why you are getting agitated. Remember, they are not mind readers, let them know what you are thinking to help your situation together be purposeful and effective. Otherwise, they get frustrated too, and this causes more problems for everyone.

## Be Aware of Your Triggers

Whenever there are relationship problems, it is always easiest to point the finger at the other person, but this does not fix, change, or solve anything. It leaves everything exactly as it is which, continues to create problems in relationships. Every situation takes at least two people to engage. Notice what you are bringing to the table and if it is elevating the relationship or bringing the relationship down. If you notice the same problem happening, the first thing to do is become aware of what you are bringing to the problem energetically. What energetic baggage and patterns are you bringing and how is this affecting the relationship?

It is extremely important to be aware of what baggage you are bringing to your communications with others. Can you hear what they are saying or are you blocked by your experiences from that day? Are you able to speak clearly or is something energetically keeping you from being able to? Many times, people trigger something within you that they did not realize was a trigger because it is not a trigger with anyone else. If you keep triggering the same thing with each other what is the pattern, the energy exchange, and how can you change it?

It is your job and responsibility to energetically be aware of what you are holding onto and why. If you do not know what the problem is how can you fix it or expect others to be able to help you with it? When you are upset, notice what is really going on, and why are you really mad? What is at the core of what is bothering you? When else does this get you upset? The moment you are aware of what the problem is, it is ready to be healed. Every time.

## *Built Up Baggage*

Everyone has a place where you store your baggage to deal with later, but when is later? Usually, it just builds and eventually surfaces as displaced anger. Notice where you intentionally store the things that bother you in your body. It is usually a specific location like in your throat, chest, or stomach. Where do you store your anger, stress, and frustration? How do you typically let it go, or does it stay dormant until you explode?

At some point you will not be able to push it down any longer and you will find yourself literally exploding in a fury of anger. It could be over something small or something that has nothing to do with what you are really upset about. This is not okay for you or the other person, ever. Especially if you take it out on someone else and it has nothing to do with them. Anger can fuel you but it most often destroys you and your relationships. Regain control over your energy by letting all the anger go and refilling that space with things that will nourish, support, and balance your being.

## *Speak the Truth*

In all relationships it is extremely important for you to speak the truth, whether that truth is known by many or a personal truth. At some level, people always know when you are not speaking the truth and this will always come back to you in some way. Remember, what you do to others always comes back to you.

By speaking the truth and surrounding yourself with people that speak the truth, you will feel free. Make sure that you are not lying to yourself either; this is usually categorized as denial. Surrounding yourself with people that tell the truth will lead to satisfying relationships that make you feel safe and appreciated. The more that you are in these types of relationships, the less you are interested in surrounding yourself with people that lie or people that you feel you have to lie to. The truth always sets you free, literally.

Trust is key in every relationship as an essential part of the relationship's foundation. If the relationship has no trust, it is doomed. No matter how hard it may seem to tell the truth, a life of not being able to speak the truth is harder. The consequences of not speaking your truth physically appear in your throat area. Find a way to speak your truth, always.

## Omitting the Truth

If you omit the truth or an important detail from your story, that is still considered lying. Some would disagree because they believe they are not telling all of the truth to help the other person, but really they are selfishly protecting themselves. The reality is that you are not speaking the truth when you omit any piece of the truth. You are telling a version of the truth, which becomes a story and is a lie. ANY deviation from the truth is a lie. At some level, people can always tell when you are keeping something from them even if they choose not to call you out on it. Something that is small or trivial becomes the huge elephant in the room, especially as time goes by and it will harm the relationship.

It becomes difficult to keep track of your lies. You may forget the details you said, what you are leaving out, or what you told to different people. It is always easier to tell the truth than to keep track of your lies. People may not be happy with what you have to tell them, but they are more understanding if they hear the truth the first time, instead of after you tell them a lie and then you try to fix it later.

The best practice is not to do anything you are afraid to tell the other person about in your relationship, whether that is a friend, family member, or a significant other. If you think that you have to keep something from someone, take a closer look at why you did what you did. Why would you do something to intentionally hurt someone else? Why do you feel the need to lie? More importantly, was it worth it? What are you really afraid of?

## Once You Have Lied

When you do not tell the truth, it energetically eats at you. You will feel uncomfortable and unsettled until it is resolved. There is no magic way to resolve it except not to lie in the first place. However, once you have lied, at some point you have to tell the person or people involved the truth. This is the only way to clear and free the energy. Remember, this is hard to do for a reason, so you do not do it again.

Once a lie is out there, there is no pulling it back or a quick fix to make you feel better. Trust is broken, feelings get hurt, and people feel angry. Remember, it is always harder to tell the truth later, especially when that moment has moved on. There is always a perfect moment to tell the truth, and if you do not do it in that moment it feels awkward, strange, and difficult. When someone gives you the opening to tell the truth, always do it in that moment. Always. Going back to them and telling them later when they already gave you an opportunity is very difficult for a reason, so you remember to tell the truth going forward. Once you tell them the truth, what they decide to do with it is up to them. At this point you should stop judging yourself and work on energetically freeing yourself.

Most people do not have a tolerance for people that lie. If you find yourself in a relationship where you are telling the lies or receiving them, ask yourself why you keep putting yourself in this situation and how setting boundaries can help you. Lies have a way of taking over and creating a life of their own, where no one feels safe, loved, or appreciated. If you find you cannot tell someone the truth, then the best practice is to not be in a relationship with them. On the flipside, if you find yourself in a relationship with someone who is always lying, why do you stay in that relationship?

## When You Cannot Share

Another time people often tell lies is when they are protecting information that they actually cannot share or do not want to share with someone. Sometimes, people do not realize they are crossing a line with you when they ask how much something costs, intimate relationship details that have no bearing on them, or juicy information on someone else. In these situations, instead of lying and making up excuses tell them, "I am sorry. This has nothing to do with you, and I cannot talk about it."

They should respect you not being able to or not wanting to share information with them that does not affect them. If they do not, then question what intimate details they are sharing about you with others. If someone respects you, they will not make you say things that are not yours to share. Do not let people put you in a place where you cannot tell the truth about something you cannot share.

If you are in a conversation with a friend, family member, or colleague and something is not their business, it is always best to say, "I am not able to talk about this with you." That may cause some uneasiness and force you to draw boundaries, but energetically it is better than lying to them.

## Communicating in an Argument

Arguments usually happened because a trigger is pulled in one of the participants. Possible triggers could be the baggage that you are carrying is literally ready to explode, stressful events that elevate a situation, being unhappy, or a communication problem. The communication that leads to the argument could be a misunderstanding, intentional, from believing the other person is wrong, you are right, or perhaps it is from not saying something that should have been said.

Arguments can change a relationship drastically. People may become passive, aggressive, or distant after a fight. It can make someone feel as though they cannot express their concerns or feelings and then they begin to stifle them until they literally explode. They can also push people away, but if done in a respectful way and with a higher purpose, arguments can create positive changes in a relationship. It is easier to be aware of what you are saying and doing than to fix it later. It just is.

## How to Prevent an Argument

One of the best ways to prevent an argument is to let someone know when something is bothering you, instead of letting it grow into something bigger than it really was originally. This means address something as it is happening, if possible, instead of waiting for later. Often, when you wait to tell them, they will want an example. Usually, you cannot give them one because you have moved on from the incident and only remember your anger or frustration, and this will cause more problems.

The purpose in telling someone how you feel in the moment is so that you can purposefully create a positive change in the relationship in that moment. If you do not want something to keep happening, let them know what is bothering you and what would be helpful. For example, if you are mad at the way someone is treating you, it is best to let them know that this is not okay when it is actually happening. You can tell them with "I feel," statements. When you are telling someone how you feel, they cannot say, "No, you do not feel that way." They are not you. How can they ever possibly know exactly how you are feeling? Since they cannot know how you are feeling, it is very important that you let people know when they are doing something that upsets, bothers, or makes you uncomfortable. If you tell someone how you feel about something early on, it is much easier to keep that from becoming a difficult pattern to break later.

Whatever you do, do not sleep on it when you are angry. If you can only begin to discuss a situation, then do what you can do before you go to sleep. As you sleep at night in the dark, negative thoughts can get crazy and out of control. There is a reason people say not go to bed mad. At least let go of your anger and frustration before you lay down.

## Energy Awareness During an Argument

Whenever there is an argument, it is always best to pause and breathe before you respond, especially in an intense argument or an argument that you have had before. The only way to create a change is to be clear about how you are using your energy and how you can create a positive shift in this moment for this situation. Typically, when you are in a fight, you like to respond as quickly as possible and with whatever thoughts first come to your mind without even thinking about what you are saying. Usually, the intent is to hurt the other person because you are hurting, or to hurt them before they hurt you. However, this approach usually leads to regretting what you said and having to apologize, sometimes profusely. Sometimes, the damage from the words said in a fight linger for days, weeks, years, and in worst-case situations, into other-life experiences.

Whether the fight is small or big, it puts energetic blocks into the relationship. Everyone deals with fights differently. It is based on their childhood, their other-life experiences, and on the relationship with the person fighting with them. For example, you will fight differently with a sibling or significant other than with a co-worker or your boss.

Be purposeful and aware of what you are saying and your energy. You may need to do the exercises in chapter seven before you talk to them. Make sure that you are sticking to the topic at hand. Do not ever bring up past arguments, they are over and done. Rehashing them just causes more arguments when you are learning to prevent them. Learn from your past arguments, make resolutions you can both honor, and move forward. Whenever you come up with a resolution, stick with it or adjust as necessary on both parts. This can create a shift in a positive direction and prevent future arguments.

## Know When to Walk Away Purposefully

You know when an argument is brewing. You always get to decide, am I going to participate, is this worth participating in, can this be resolved now, or should we walk away and think about this first? These are the things you should immediately analyze energetically before you speak to respond.

Sometimes, you just have to walk away. Not angrily, but with the intention and mutual agreement to work on this later when everyone has had time to do some letting go, cool down, and come back with a way to resolve the situation. If you find you are not making any progress or are at a stalemate, give yourself and everyone involved time to let go, recenter, and come back with a way to make a change. The purpose of an argument is not to be mad at each other forever, rather it is a way to create a positive change in your relationship so you do not get to this point again.

When you come back together an hour, two hours later, or whatever time you both agree to, the purpose is to both come back with a way to resolve this. Make sure you are both bringing to the table something that you can do and something they can do to prevent this problem from arising again. This will involve compromise on both of your parts. Sometimes, one person may compromise more than another and that is okay as long as it is not the same person always giving up more. It really does have to be equal or there will be bigger problems in the relationship.

## How to Move Forward After an Argument

Sometimes, an argument happens. Hopefully, you spoke calmly, purposefully, and used "I feel," statements to speak your point. Ideally, everyone has learned what to do, what not to do in this relationship, and how to communicate with each other.

Make sure you are honoring any changes you said that you would make and nicely let the other person know if they are not.

For example, you can say, "Remember we talked about this, please _____." The purpose is not to get into a fight again, rather to prevent a fight and honor the changes that everyone agreed to. Sometimes, people are not aware that they are slipping into an old pattern; they need a gentle reminder.

The goal is to be happy, not angry, bitter, and scheming ways to punish the other person. If you are in an argument, make sure it is productive and not pointless. Your intention should be to move forward together in a new way, not to keep having the same fight continually. That is the definition of insanity, to keep doing the same thing over and over again and expecting different results.

Almost always, there is some energetic healing to do after a fight. It is important to look at what triggered you to fight or fight back. What can you let go of? What can you do differently next time to prevent this from happening? If this keeps happening, then it is time for something to really change. What is it? Make sure you are not carrying baggage from this experience around with you. It will not help you or them at any point.

Most importantly, you both have to make an agreement to not bring this fight up again in another argument. If you do, it will not bring peace, healing, or transparency. It will make you stuck, angry, and helpless because you are not moving forward from it. Whenever there is a fight, agree to move forward and not do whatever brought this problem on again. It may take baby steps at first, especially if this is an old pattern and that is okay as long as things are shifting in a positive way. The only way to go forward is to stop looking backwards.

# 4 – Drama

Drama. The word alone will stir an intense emotion in you. Everyone is exposed to it at a young age and this either pulls you into it or you run away from it when you see it a mile away. Some people believe that drama is just a part of life and others will not let it be a part of their life. Drama is a choice; you choose to create it, engage in it, or stay out of it. Learn about your role in drama, how control creates drama, and how to stop the drama in your life.

## *Understanding Your Role in Drama*

Drama happens in all settings and in all types of relationships. It happens in families, friendships, in the workplace, and in intimate relationships. It takes a lot of energy. During dramatic encounters you may experience energy highs, a sense of heightened awareness, and a lot of adrenaline. However, you cannot stay in that place energetically. It takes too much energy and you will come crashing down, just like a high from sugar, caffeine, drugs, or alcohol. Typically, you will feel drained after a dramatic encounter and it often leads you to feel like a tornado just left the room. How do you feel about drama? Do you love drama and create it, are you in the middle of it, or do you stay clear of it? What you pick from these options will help you understand, energetically, about your relationships.

## Drama Creators

When you are in a relationship with people in a "Me Mentality," you will experience drama. Part of the reason for this is because someone with a "Me Mentality," all the time or temporarily wants the attention on them. If the attention is not on them, they will almost always do something to get it back on them. Drama is a way to get attention, not necessarily good attention, but nonetheless, it gets you in the spotlight.

If you do love creating drama, one thing you will notice is that people may not trust you. They do not know when you will start a problem, how this will affect them, and what you are pulling them into. You may find that most of your relationships are short-term, and the only people that stay long-term are other people that like or tolerate drama. Although, having to constantly make new connections and friends may be exciting and can create more drama around you.

One thing to think about if you like drama is why do you like it? Here are some specific questions to help you get to the root of why you or someone in your life keeps creating drama: Where does your need for chaos and uncertainty come from? Why does this make you feel good? How do you feel when people leave? Now that you are looking at this objectively, is this something you still feel compelled to do?

Something that happens frequently with people that create drama is that they continually create the same drama-filled situations in different places. It is the same story, different setting, and new people, consistently. The only thing that changes is that each time the situation gets more intense and it creates more drama. This is happening to help you create a shift so that this place becomes so uncomfortable that you have to make a change and stop creating it. If this is happening to you, please pay attention so things can get better for you and those around you. Know that if there is a lot of drama in your life, you are engaging it, creating it, and at some level enjoying it or it would not be there. Drama is a choice, it does not just happen to you or follow you. You have to engage in it.

## Peace Makers

Peace makers want to keep the peace and often they come from families where this was a skill they learned in childhood. They may keep information from one side intentionally, they may put themselves in the middle and relay messages in an effort to keep the peace, or they alter the message and sugar coat it. All of this puts them in the middle of the fire because they are the middle person between two other people. Sometimes, they may just submit and do something they do not want to do to make someone else happy. In doing these things, they too, create drama for themselves and those around them by putting themselves in the middle of the drama. Of course, it is not as much drama as the drama creators make, but as you try to tone down the drama without removing yourself from the drama, it becomes an extension of the drama.

Trying to prevent or stop the drama still creates drama. The only way to really stop the drama is to not participate in it at all. As a true peace maker, you have a hard time just completely walking away because you truly believe your job is to help calm down the drama, even if you do not pass along the drama to the intended recipient. However, the best way to tone down the drama is to not participate in it at all.

It does not matter if you come from a small or big family, if there is drama in your family you have peace makers. Eventually, the goal is for the peace makers to realize that they really are not stopping the drama or lessening it. They are just extending it and creating more for themselves. The moment they realize that, they are free from this burden that they took upon themselves or that was forced upon them.

## Drama Avoiders

There are some people who cannot stand drama and want no part of it. They have had their fill, they know what it does, and they consciously choose not to be a part of it. Typically, they have experienced a lot of it early in their childhood, and when they see it coming they either run from it or they draw a boundary to stop it. Avoiding drama can actually create more drama, so it is not the best way to prevent drama.

Ideally, a boundary is drawn in dramatic situations because that is the best way to stop it and prevent more drama from occurring. When you run away from dramatic situations, you just keep attracting them to you because you are not dealing with them. Whatever you do not deal with in your life, you bring more of to you until you learn how to overcome it. Instead, draw boundaries and stop the drama.

## Common Ways You Engage in Drama

Regardless of how you feel about drama, you can think of examples where it has caused problems in relationships. It makes people choose sides, feel uncomfortable, and it makes things more intense than they should be. Sometimes, you may be doing something that creates drama and other times, drama may be the end result of you not doing something you should have done. Like everything else, it is important to understand how you are using your energy by engaging in drama.

### *Confrontation*

Many people will do whatever they can do to avoid confrontation. By avoiding confrontation, many small matters escalate out of control, personally and professionally. Confrontation can be a dramatic event for many people based upon their past experiences. As you are learning, it does not have to be.

If it is your job to stop things before they get out of control, then stop them. When you let things get out of control this creates unnecessary drama, especially in the work place. Confrontation does not have to be a negative thing, rather it is a way to get something back on track before it derails out of control. Instead of being afraid of telling someone how you feel, think about what will be the end result months from now when you have to tell them the issue AND that this has been going on for months. That will create more drama for everyone.

People respond based upon how you present things to them. If you present a solution to someone in a place that you are better than them, they will most likely take it in a bad, negative way, ensuring a dramatic experience for all. When you present a problem in a way that calls for everyone to come up with a resolution, it is perceived better, takes less energy, and is not dramatic.

Confrontation can be positive. It is extremely important how you relay the message. Be factual, be aware of the energy in the room, stay on topic, and whenever possible ask for their feedback on how they can be accountable and get things back on track.

### Being Too Busy

Being too busy is actually a way you create drama for yourself. When you are too busy, you do not have time to sit still and process what is really going on in your life. If you do not like your environment to be quiet, notice that the noise brings you comfort because it distracts you and prevents you from being alone with yourself.

When you are busy it keeps you from having to deal with the things in your life that you do not want to deal with, or it makes you feel important because you are so busy. Either way, the end result is the same. By not making a quiet time for yourself to process the things you have to deal with in your life, they get bigger and bigger until you are forced to deal with them. Constantly thinking and doing creates drama for you.

It is important in your busy lifestyle that you take a break and just be. This allows you to step away from all the craziness around you, and for you to reconnect with yourself and what is most important to you. When you take time to be, you will find solutions to the things you are struggling with, you will make time to connect with your intuition, which is really important if you only connect with it in your dreams, and you will feel happier and more peaceful.

Society has you plugged in constantly even on vacations by sharing your fun times on social media or with others not with you. Take time to unplug, put your phone on silent, and in an opposite part of your house when you can. Check your emails at scheduled times and give yourself time off from them. Spend time in nature just being, not always doing an activity. If you cannot sit still with yourself for at least five minutes, this has to become your priority.

You are not meant to go all the time. You are not a machine. You are a being, a being that likes balance in all things. When the scales tip too much in one way, things will happen to get you back to your center. Drama happens less when you are balanced in your life.

## *Control*

Control creates problems and drama in relationships. When one person is trying to control someone else, that creates tension not only between the people directly involved, but also with the people watching. No one wants to watch someone lose their power and be helpless, it makes them feel uncomfortable and they may try and stand up for the person.

Relationships may begin in a way that one person controls the other and everyone is okay with that. However, as people change they will resent always being in charge or always being told what to do. In these relationships, there is a lot of drama because someone is exerting their power and someone is losing their power.

In controlling relationships, people use control to avoid dealing with their problems. Instead, they focus on shaping someone to be how they want them to be and this takes the focus off of what they are missing in their own life. This allows them to literally place someone in a box of what is acceptable and what is not. When the other person can no longer stand to be controlled, the controller has a choice to change or usually, the relationship will end. It is not a matter of if this will happen, rather a matter of when. At some point, the person being controlled will have enough and try to break free.

Usually, if someone is letting you control them, this is a red flag for you. Something bigger is going on that you are not aware of and may not be aware of for months, years, or decades. When someone lets you control them and they hand their power over to you, you really should ask them why they are doing it. Most people will not hand over their power without a fight, so it is important to really pay attention and see what behaviors are happening in their life. It may be something like being immature or ungrounded. It can also be something bigger like a dependency on drugs, alcohol, or coming from an abused relationship.

If you are controlling someone or being controlled, stop and look at what is really going on. In the end, you will not be happy in either position and you will grow to resent the other person. The more balanced a relationship is, the happier everyone in it is and there is no need for control or drama. Instead of trying to fix someone else, focus on fixing yourself.

## Manipulation

Manipulation is the most typical way used to get control over someone. You play on their fears, their emotions, and even their love. The problem with manipulation is that when you make people do things they do not want to do, they end up resenting you. The more you manipulate them, the more they resent you until one day they literally explode and cannot take anymore. In the end, instead of bringing them closer to you, you push them far, far away.

### *Manipulating Someone*

Manipulation eventually creates the exact opposite result of what you would like to create, so why even do it? You know that trying to control someone else does not work long-term and that at some point it will back fire. It is just a matter of when and what you will lose when this happens.

The next time you think you are going to lie and manipulate a situation to get what you want out of someone, stop. Remind yourself that you will not get the end result you want this way long-term, and if you take a moment while this is happening to look back at past experiences, you will see that this is true. Instead, use you words in a clear way and tell the other person what you would like from them and why. Let them know your fears and see where you can meet each other in the middle.

Relationships always flow better and have happier endings when you stop the drama and come up with a solution together.

## *Being Manipulated*

If you are the one being manipulated, once you are aware of what is happening and the power that you are losing, the question becomes why are you continuing to be a part of this pattern? As you are manipulated, your anger grows every time you give up something that matters to you for the other person. You will also notice that when you give up something for them, they want something else right away. There is always something else for you to give up. Eventually, your anger and frustrations grow pushing you to a boiling point where you are forced to stop and reclaim your self-worth and power. This can take years if you do not stop it right away. Notice the next time you give up something, they are back pretty quickly with something else they want you to do for them, and it is usually not what you want to do.

If you do not catch and stop this behavior right away, you have to take a step back from the situation and see what is really happening. What pattern have you created? Why are you giving over your power and more importantly, how long have you been doing it? Chances are you are going back to your childhood and other-life experiences. Imagine that you are watching this whole situation on a television show rerun. What is the pattern that keeps happening? Who is it happening with and how are these relationships connected? How do you feel before, during, and after? Why do you let this keep happening to you? What can you do to regain your power?

Once you have decided that you are done being manipulated, the first step is to draw a boundary with that person. This is how you start to reclaim your power back. If they do not respect the boundary, they do not respect you. If they do not respect you, there is no point in a relationship with them because they will just continue to hurt you. This all just leads to a lot of unnecessary drama and pain in your life. The question is not if you will stop it, it is a matter of when and how much you give up before you reach this point. It is all up to you. Do you choose balanced relationships or dramatic ones?

## *Stop the Drama*

You may not believe you have a choice of engaging in or preventing drama, but you do. You get to choose how you spend your energy in every moment. Do not engage if you do not want to be involved. You always have the right to say, "No, thank you." Then, you can peacefully walk away and let go of any anger and frustration as you leave the situation.

The biggest way you can stop drama in your life is to prevent problems before they grow out of control. The earlier you tell someone about a problem, the better. Remember to say it in a way that they will hear you so that a change can be made. The more balanced the situation, the less room there is for drama to appear and take control. If you see the drama starting and you cannot stop it, then you can choose not to be a part of it. Do not put your energy into it when they try and pull you in. Just imagine giving it back to them gently and saying, "No, thank you."

When you are in a relationship with one or two people in a "Me Mentality," you may notice a lot of drama. They are focused on themselves, and when they are not the focus, they will make themselves the focus. Often, they have a lot of the same problems over and over again in different situations. Whenever this is happening, look big picture, see what the problem is, and how you are supporting it. If you are in the "Me Mentality," take a look and see what you can do differently and how you can make a change for those around you by being more we focused. If you are in the "We Mentality," take a step back, look big picture, and become aware of why the drama is happening and why you are a part of it.

You choose to engage, create, and continue drama in your life. The more drama you have around you, the more you create in all your relationships. When drama no longer supports you, stop engaging in it. Your energy will instantly feel lighter. Read more about ways to bring balance back into your relationships in the next chapter.

# 5 – Creating Balance in Your Relationships

Relationships are not often a smooth, effortless ride. They take work, compromise, respect, and love. Relationships do require work on everyone's part, and one of the most important things to do in a relationship is to make sure there is balance. When a relationship has balance, people are happy. Think about it. How many people that are in balanced relationships complain to you with their relationship problems? How many people do you know in balanced relationships?

Usually, you hear about problems in relationships because they are unbalanced and the people are looking for a way to make them functional. There are things you can do to create balance in all of your relationships, but remember, if someone does not respect you, you cannot fix that. You can create new relationships though, with people who will respect you. The sections in this chapter will help you create balance in your relationships by creating boundaries, breaking down walls, being aware of your energy, and being aware of your role in your relationships.

## *Create Boundaries*

You cannot change people and their behaviors. You can only control you. That person may change, but it is because they decided to make that change. Even in leaving a relationship, you cannot force someone to change, that change has to come from within them. You can change yourself and how you deal or decide not to deal with their behaviors, but you cannot change other people. Whether a spouse, a friend, or a family member what you see is what you get. This either draws you to them or repels you away.

This is where boundaries come in. If you do not like what someone is doing or how they are treating you, it is time to create a boundary, and in some situations, multiple boundaries. Even if you have to be around people in certain situations at work, you do not have to let them energetically control you. You can create boundaries and balance in those relationships.

## Understanding Boundaries

Boundaries protect your energy and your relationship. They let people know what behavior is okay and what is not. A lot of times, people do not know what the boundaries are because you have not set any. What is a problem for you may be okay with someone else. Many relationship problems stem from people being upset at how they are being treated, but they continually let it happen. How do people know what is okay and what is not if you do not set boundaries?

When you set boundaries for old relationship patterns people will most likely challenge them. They either want to see how firm you are going to be on that boundary, or they do not care at all and want to do what they want to do. If they are just testing to see how firm the boundary is and they are able to adhere to the boundary, that shows that they at least respect and want to be in the relationship. They may mess up a few times, but keep being firm and they will respect the boundary. If they just want to do what they want to do regardless of how that affects you, it becomes time to see how they should still be a part of your life. If they do need to be a part of your life, then the boundaries become very firm, something that limits your exposure to them.

Of course there may be people that you absolutely have to be around because you work with them or have some activity that forces you to be around them. Then, you set a different boundary, one that is about not letting them affect your energy. They can do whatever they want energetically, but you imagine their energy bouncing right off of you and back to them. You do not do this in a mean or malicious way, rather an indifferent way. You simply do not let their energy imprint on you or have an effect on you. When their energy comes at you simply say, "No, thank you." Imagine their energy gently going right back to them because it is their energy and they can have it back.

## How to Set Boundaries

Sometimes, you keep finding yourself pulled into a relationship that you know is bad and dysfunctional for you. You try to distance yourself and ignore them, and before you know it they have pulled you in again. How does this keep happening?

You let them. They know your weak points, you have told them what they are. They know how to get to you, and they do it over and over again because you have let them. They know you, so they know how to manipulate your energy which literally gives them the keys to control you. Now that you are aware of it and are no longer interested in this dance, it is time to change your pattern with a boundary.

You do not want to throw daggers, put up blocks or walls, or do anything to call their attention to you in a negative way. This is actually more work for you, and as you have noticed, it is not effective in balancing the relationship. It can actually bring you some bad karma. Instead, you do not take on their energy. Whatever they say, do, or however they try to pull you in, you simply and gently push the energy away and say, "No, thank you." You do not give them their energy back in any different way than how they gave it to you. You simply return it to them and move on from a place of love and peace. It is like you are a mirror and it bounces off of you and right back onto them in the same way they gave it to you.

They will not know how to respond to this and they may keep trying to find some way to engage with you for a bit. After all, this is a long established pattern, almost a game that they do with you. It is fun for them or they would not keep doing it. If you keep giving their energy back to them every time without taking it in, they will stop. Think of a child doing bad things to get attention, the more you engage, the worse they get. It is the same with someone you no longer would like to engage with. They keep doing things to try and engage you. Once you stop playing, it is no longer fun and they will move on.

## Respect Boundaries

Boundary setting absolutely goes both ways, so make sure you respect the boundaries that others set with you. Boundaries are typically set to let you know how to treat someone, basically, what is okay to do and what is not. If someone is setting a boundary, they have a reason for it. Something has happened that has made this boundary important, whether it was something someone else has done or something you have done.

Respect other's boundaries just as you would like them to respect yours. If you do not respect someone's boundary, what does that tell them? It tells them that you do not respect them and that whatever you want is more important than the needs of the relationship. It also signals a "Me Mentality," in a relationship. At some point, the boundary will become releasing the relationship and any energy attached to it.

## *Break Down Any Walls*

A boundary should never be a wall. It does not really work and it takes a ton of energy to hold it up. How can you truly be in any relationship if you have energetically built a castle with a moat around you and they cannot get in? When you are emotionally unavailable in any of your relationships, the other people know. They may be okay with it at first because they are also emotionally unavailable, and they can stay emotionally unavailable too, or they want to fix you. Either way, this leads to problems. How can two emotionally unavailable people be in a relationship together for very long? The relationship would become stagnant. If the person wants you to be more open, and you do not want to be, you will reach a standstill.

## Let Love In

Something to think about in your relationships is what is in charge. Is it fear or love? If fear is in charge, you may find yourself constantly building those walls to keep people at bay. However, when you keep people at a distance, it affects the whole relationship. It makes it feel lonely and empty. The essence of why people are in relationships is to love and be loved, to feel connected, and to not feel alone or separated. As people realize that the relationship is one-sided or unfulfilling, they will leave.

Relationships should be equal and if they are not, building a wall will not help your relationship. The more relationships you have where you feel nurtured and supported, the more you can reciprocate that to others because it feels good; if your pattern has been building walls, you will not feel a need to build them. When you feel love, you share that energy with everyone around you and it brings that energy back to you. You cannot do that with walls standing between you and the others in your relationships.

Break the walls down and if you cannot do that in your relationship, then you have to look at why you are in it. What is the point? If you surround yourself with people and you do not let them in, you will feel lonely and isolated. By breaking down the walls and letting people into your heart, you will feel love and connected with them again.

## Let People In

Part of being in relationships with people is to actually let them into your life. If you do not let them in, you are not honoring yourself or them. You are not protecting yourself either. Instead, you are creating surface relationships that will not bring you or them long-term happiness. You may even find that the relationships feel empty and they make you feel even more alone. Empty relationships are not a replacement for relationships with people that will love, nurture, and support you.

When it comes to romantic relationships or amazing friendships, do not settle. You either have a connection with someone or you do not. If you try to make things work when you are not fully vested or available, it is not fair to you or the other person. You will just make yourselves miserable and you will find you are still not letting people in.

If you look back at who has hurt you in the past, it was people that did not truly love you. Instead of creating more relationships that are the same, let go of your fears and see yourself surrounded in relationships where people truly do love and support you emotionally, as you do likewise to them. Every time you feel the fear of being hurt or abandoned reappear, remember this vision of being surrounded by people that love you, and then really let these people into your life.

Surround yourself with people that you enjoy being around, that you can let in, and that you feel safe with. Let your relationships be filled with love and compassion, not a fear of getting hurt. You will find that when you do not truly let people in, the person you are hurting the most is yourself. You are not meant to be alone. You are a being of light and love and you can attract light and love into your life. It is the best way to create happy, balanced, fulfilling relationships.

## *Be Aware of Your Energy*

Whatever is happening in your life, in that moment you choose how to respond to it. If you continue to have the same problems in your relationships whether they are at work, or with family, or friends, it becomes time to look at what you are doing. Whenever something is happening often, it is because you are creating it. If you are unhappy with the same pattern being created in your life in different places, then look objectively at what you are doing and why you keep doing it. Once you are aware of what you are creating, then you have to change the pattern.

Typically, when something happens, you respond immediately in the way you always have. This is a problem when you do not like the way that things keep turning out. Think about it, if you keep doing things the way you always have, you will continue to have the same results. Often times, you learn how to handle stress, frustration, anger, confrontation, etc., in the same way your parents and caretakers did. After all, they were your early life teachers. Think about how the people that took care of you as a child responded to the things you are having a problem with. Did they respond the same way? If not, who did? You learned this way of coping from someone. How did the people respond to them when they acted this way? Are you experiencing the same thing?

In order to change this, you have to pay attention to what you are doing with your energy when something is happening that you do not like. For example, if you feel like people are out to get you, you are probably doing things to push them away without even being aware that you are doing it. This behavior will either make people want to get away from you, or it will make them want to get rid of you. If you create drama and make people feel bad, you may discover that your relationships are constantly in chaos. However, if you pause before you respond and try to respond in the best way possible for everyone involved, you will find that people will respond better to you.

Remember, what you do to others, you do to yourself. If you try to isolate someone, you isolate yourself. If you try to control someone, you control yourself because that takes a lot of energy and you will not feel like you can be free. Try pausing before you respond. In our society, everything feels like it has to be done so quickly, but if you keep responding quickly, you are responding without thinking. You will keep doing what you have always done, and chances are there are things about this that you are ready to change.

## Spend Time with People You Love

The people that are around you are a reflection of you because like attracts like. If you surround yourself with people that bring you down, they bring down your energy as well. If you do not like the people that you are spending time with, the next step is to take a look at why you are not surrounding yourself with people that you enjoy and that enjoy you as well? Why do you surround yourself with people that you do not like? Does it make you feel better or worse? Why? Are you happy with this or would you like to change it? You choose the friends, family, and significant other in your life. Choose wisely because if you are not happy with the people in your life, it brings your energy down.

Surround yourself with people that you love to be around and likewise, love to be around you. When you surround yourself with people that you love and enjoy being around, you lift up each other's energy level. These are the moments that bring you peace, happiness, and joy. In these moments, you spread light and love to all those around you, and you are making a difference in the world. They are the moments you look back at and smile.

## Trust Your Instincts

One of the most important things you can do in a relationship is to pay attention to your instincts and actually follow them. You always have a feel for someone when you first meet them, trust that. Usually, when a relationship is bad, people will remember that they did not have a good instinct with that person and they ignored it anyway. Stop ignoring your instincts and start following them. They are a tool for you, so pay attention and follow your guidance to make things easier on yourself.

Do not go to other people to see what they think of someone. They have different karma with them, relationship patterns, and beliefs than you do, so their guidance will probably not be right for you, but for them. Pay attention to what you feel and know that you are being guided in a way that someone else may not be. The guidance you receive will have a special meaning for you.

There is only so much time in a day. Spend it with people you enjoy being around instead of people that you feel you have to be around. Do not ignore your instincts. They are your compass to help you know who to connect with and who to stay away from. As people shift, you will be guided to reach out to them or to give them space. If you are thinking about someone, there is always a reason. Make sure you follow that instinct and reach out to them.

## *Your Role in Relationships*

No person or title alone should define who you are. You are complex and full of possibilities. Take time to figure out: what your role is, if you like it or want to change it, and what do you want your role to be in your relationships. Your relationships are a reflection of what is happening within yourself. If they feel crazy and out of control, it is time to look at what is happening within you. You create your life in every moment.

Be aware of how you treat yourself and how you let people treat you. If you do not treat yourself from a place of love, others will not either. Notice the words you use in your mind towards yourself as well. Stop any endless, negative chatter. Instead, focus on your strengths, your purpose, and the things that make you happy. If you find yourself in a relationship that is pulling you down and making you miserable, why are you staying? What is it doing to your energy and in turn to the energy of those around you? You do get to choose how you respond to the people in your life, draw boundaries if they must stay, and let them go if they can go.

Your energy, stress, and being out of balance all take a toll on your health, which is directly your relationship with yourself. If you are not taking care of yourself, no one else can take care of you either. They cannot fix you. On an airplane, you have to put the oxygen on yourself before you can take care of others. In order to create balanced relationships you have to be in a good place first. Then the relationships follow. Always. Notice that when you reach a breaking point in any relationship, the first relationship to evaluate is your relationship with yourself. This sets the stage for all of your relationships; how you treat yourself is how others treat you too. If you do not like what is happening in your relationships, look within and see what you are creating, and then make the necessary changes to create happy, nurturing, and fulfilling relationships.

# 6 – Setting Yourself Free

Not all relationships are meant to last a lifetime, only a few do. All relationships have their own time and purpose. This is not necessarily what you think they should be or how you would like them to be. Enjoy your relationships when you are in them and if they come to an end, it is important to set yourself free. As time passes, you understand why things happen when they do and this includes the relationships ending in your life.

Relationships are heavily influenced from the past as you read in chapter two. Other lives, past experiences, perceptions from childhood, and what society says you should be doing all heavily influence the relationships in your life right now. As you let go of the things you are holding onto and move forward in your life, you will notice the people in your life shifting. Perhaps a good friend is no longer a fit, as the perspective you once shared, is no longer true for one or both of you. Significant others sometimes shift as well, when the relationship no longer feels equal, healthy, or right.

Often, when a relationship is over, it does not happen overnight. Repeated events lead to the end of every relationship. You put a lot of thought into leaving a relationship. Not just because of what it will do to the other person, but because of what it will do to you too.

You know when a relationship is done. You feel it in every fiber of your being. Before this point, you feel it building slowly, but you are not ready for it to be over. You will try and make changes and do what you can to make the relationship work again. Once you know without a doubt that the relationship is finished, every moment you stay, you are angry and frustrated. The sooner you let this go, the freer you will feel, but ending a relationship is a process. The process is different for each relationship and what you are holding onto from that relationship. The focus of this chapter is to help you let a relationship that is ending, or has ended, go.

## *Why Relationships End*

Relationships end when they have served their purpose. Sometimes, you initiate it. Other times, it feels like it is happening to you which means that you have created this subconsciously. Nothing randomly happens in your life, everything has a purpose and you have agreed to it or it would not happen. Things are always shifting, and perhaps the relationship is not necessary anymore, it is not functional or healthy, or it is no longer a fit with where you are going. Whatever needed to be done and healed in this relationship in this life is complete and it is time to move on, ideally from a place of love and peace. When the experience is complete there is usually an assortment of feelings that come along with it.

If you are the person leaving the relationship, you have thought about this for some time. Rarely, does a relationship just end overnight. Usually, there is a trigger that keeps happening and no matter what you try and do differently, the end result is the same. One day, enough is enough, and you decide to leave the relationship. Chances are it will not be easy, as it is a different journey for everyone. However, if you are leaving, you have reached the pivotal moment where it is harder to stay than to make this change. You need to be free, now.

On the flip side, if you are the person being left, chances are you are surprised. Even if they have told you what is not working and that the relationship will end if things do not change, it always still comes as a surprise. For some reason, you did not think it would happen. Maybe, they have threatened to leave before and did not. Perhaps, they have been talking about it for so long and not taking any action, so you did not think it was going to happen. You knew at some level this relationship ending was a possibility, but the moment it happens, you will most likely be in shock anyhow. Remember, people mean what they say. Leaving a relationship takes time because it is a big change for everyone and no matter how dysfunctional the relationship is, it creates sadness on both sides. Often, you are most afraid of the change that ending this relationship will bring into your life.

## *Let Yourself Feel*

It is important that you let yourself feel whatever emotions are coming up. Truly feel them and then let them go. If you do not feel them you will find yourself burying them in your body to deal with later. It is best to deal with your feelings now, not later. The power is in this moment. Feel them, let them go, and refill your being with love.

Always try and deal with the emotions you are feeling instead of energetically storing them in your body. Where are the places in your body that you normally store your anger, sadness, and fears? Are you storing them or letting them go? Give yourself time to heal. This may mean time alone or supportive time with others. No matter how you are feeling, the best way to get through this is to feel it and not block it, cover it up, or ignore it. Take time to process. Look objectively at what happened, where it went wrong, and how you contributed to it ending. This is important to prevent you from unconsciously recreating the same pattern in your next relationship.

### Your Fears

Fears will appear and if you are not aware of what you are focusing on and analyzing, they will become your focus and they will energetically hold you prisoner. Your biggest fear is often the fear of being alone. That fear is followed by over-analyzing if you doing the right thing. You may find yourself in a downward spiral trying to figure out what you could have done differently to have a different ending and to not be alone. Remember, you are never truly alone. You are a being of light and love and you can return to the ball of light in any moment.

This relationship ending does not mean you are alone. It is all in what you focus on. Focus on creating positive, healing, loving, and peaceful relationships instead of just trying to fill the void with other people, things, and events. You can also return to the light and be grateful.

## Return to the Light

Love conquers all fears, even your fear of being alone. Fears are an illusion. They are darkness, an absence of light, and they are not real. Ever. You choose to give them power or to make them disappear in every moment. Fears always disappear in the light. It is as if you are entering a dark room and you turn the light switch on. Just as the darkness disappears in the light, your fears do as well.

If your fears start to take over, return to the light. Remember, the light is how we visually connect with God, Love, Universe, Source, or whatever you would like to call it. You can stand under a light in your house or stand under the sunlight outside. When you focus on the light, your fears and the darkness have no choice but to disappear. Love is real, it is powerful, and it is the truth. Love is all there is. Love conquers all and that includes your fears.

## *Be Grateful*

You can also let your fears go and focus on what you are grateful for in this moment. What makes you happy in this moment? It can be a smell in the air, the sun shining, a comfy chair, a good book, whatever it is, be grateful for it through your whole being. Feel that grateful feeling from the top of your head, all the way down to your feet, and into the Earth. You may have to do this several times and what you are grateful for will change in each moment. Just make sure you are truly grateful for whatever it is, or it will not help you redirect your energy from a place of fear to a place of love and appreciation.

## **Feeling Guilty**

Whether you left the relationship or feel that you were left, there is usually some guilt. You may feel guilty that you stayed way longer than you wanted to because you felt like you had to make it work, and you wasted time for both of you because it ended anyhow. Perhaps, you feel guilty because someone has left you once or several times, and you did not make the changes you were told to make.

There are so many things your mind can over-analyze and that you can feel guilty about. This leads to judging yourself for what happened and what went wrong, but that does not help anyone. It actually prevents you both from moving forward because it keeps your energy in the past. The question becomes, what are you letting have power over you and why? If this over-analyzing and feeling guilty does not make you feel better, why keep doing it? It almost becomes a way to punish yourself for not making it work. Honestly, if you are feeling an energetic pull to leave a relationship and the signs are all around you, then it is time to let it go. You are being guided, listen. It is time to free yourself and the other person. You had your relationship, it lasted as long as it was supposed to, and you learned and healed what you could. When nothing you both are doing anymore works no matter how hard you try, then that is your red flag saying that something has to change.

In this day and age, the romantic notion of being with a spouse or friend for sixty years is as realistic as having the same job your whole life and living in your first house until you die. It is possible and fabulous if you have an immediate connection with "The One," that you cannot imagine your life without, and it lasts a lifetime, but chances are this was not that relationship because it ended. Most people do not pay attention to their energy connections with others and they make the relationship work until it gets too hard or something that appears better comes along.

The vast majority are not wanting, looking for, or waiting for an instant, deep, "The One," connection. They just settle for whatever makes sense in that moment and this is why so many relationships are ending. Instead of feeling guilty, be aware of who you are surrounding yourself with and why. Notice that when you are happy, you spread that around you. Stop feeling guilty and start making changes within yourself. Begin by paying attention to how you spend your energy and who you really would like to spend your energy with. You only have so much time, stop settling, feeling guilty, and make your time count.

Guilt makes you feel like you should have done something different, tried harder, or been better. If you were supposed to have done something a certain way, you would have. Let it go. Be free. You cannot change what happened, you can however, change what you will do going forward.

## Feeling Sad

No matter how you have felt about the relationship while you were in it, you will be sad and you may even question why it is ending and why it had to be this way. You will question and try to over-analyze every part of the relationship and your role in it. Sometimes, you may even find yourself going back to how things were in the beginning, glossing over how things really have been, and how long it has been since you truly enjoyed being with this person.

Feeling sad is normal until you are at peace with ending the relationship. If you need to cry, then cry. Whether you are saying goodbye to a friend or a significant other, they made an impact in your life. You had a connection and you have some wonderful memories. When you cry, use this as a healing cry. Let go of whatever fears, anger, or guilt that you are holding onto. Notice where you feel that emotion in your body, let it go, and refill that area with an "I am" statement that most supports that area. Then fill your whole being with an "I am" statement like, "I am free." It has to be something that will help you move forward and reprogram the energy that you have been holding onto. When it comes to relationships, the best "I am" statements are things like: "I am free." "I am safe." "I am whole." "I am love." More detailed energy work to help you move forward is in the next chapter.

## *Be Clear*

As relationships end, one thing that can be difficult is making your intentions clear to yourself and the other person. The more blurry the lines get, the harder the separation will become for both of you. What is okay and a last time event for you, may give hope to the other person even if you are clear with your intentions. Make sure that whatever you are doing, you are not leading them on. Think before you do. Actions often speak louder than words. They may not be seeing things as they actually are, rather how they would like them to be.

Whether it is a good friendship or an intimate relationship, when a relationship that has lasted for a long time comes to an end, people will often want to try again. Sometimes, approaching the "end" makes it seem final and intense emotionally. Fears will surface and you may feel lonely, scared, and worried this is not the right decision. For example, you may think: "What if I cannot find another person to do these things with?" "What does my life look like without them in it?" It can really make you both question what is happening and why, and inevitably, you may try again.

Trying again one more time is okay only if you really are trying again, and you must be crystal clear in your intentions. When they go back to the same behaviors, let them know that they are doing them and if you are planning on leaving because of it. Be aware of your words and actions by making sure that they are purposeful and clear so they cannot be misunderstood. Do not try to sugar coat things for the other person. It really just makes it harder for everyone else in the end. Do not give the other person false hope that things are going back to the way they were if you are still making an exit plan in your mind. This will come back to haunt you.

Most importantly, you know this person and how they will respond to you. If you know that no matter what you say, this is giving them a false hope, be aware of the extra work you are making for yourself in trying again. If you are leading the other person on to make yourself feel better, be aware of the karma you are creating for yourself with them. This can make what could have been a peaceful ending turn into an angry, bitter ending where they may feel you used them. Chances are they will use this to pull you back in again.

Be clear. Be clear with your words, your actions, and your intentions. Do not just do what is best for you. No matter how painful or hard it may seem, it really is easier to do what is best for everyone involved the first time. An ending may be sad, but it does not have to be unbearably difficult for everyone involved. That is a choice.

## *Energetically Moving Forward*

The people that support you will shift as you shift. You may find your support system has been with you all along and they will continue to support you. Other times, you may find that the people who hung around in the background are stepping up to be here for you through this. Sometimes, your old friends and support system cannot see you through this change. Then you find yourself connecting with a new support base of people going through a similar situation. No matter what, remember, you are never alone. Energetically, you are always connected.

Being in limbo makes everything seem way harder. If you cannot move forward then nothing changes. If nothing is changing you feel stuck, depressed, and you may lose sight of your purpose. When a relationship ends, whether by your choice or they leave you, it is important for you and them that you let them go. If you hang on to them and any part of your old routine together, it hurts you both energetically and it holds you both trapped. Pay attention, because the Universe constantly sends you signals, signs, and hints to let you know what to do and when to do it. The key is to pay attention and do it. Some things to help you energetically move forward are: to pay attention to what you are focusing on, become aware or your triggers, and to move forward physically and emotionally.

## Perspective and Focus

When moving on from a relationship, it is all about perspective. It really is mind over matter. What you focus on, you bring more of to you. Society says that you have to go through a pretty detailed mourning period. Grief is different for everyone. Before you leave a relationship, you already mourned it. You have been processing and planning. If you wanted to be with that person you would be and you would not have left them. Everyone says, "It is so hard." How you feel and process is actually a conscious choice. If you think it is hard, it is. What you think you create. Leaving and being left are different experiences every time. It depends on what you learned, what you have to heal, and how you are going to move forward.

Yes, you have good memories and good experiences, but the truth is that it has not been good for awhile. If it was, you would not be leaving them. Leaving a relationship does not have to be hard. It can be easier if you focus on the right things for you. Do not focus on what makes this process difficult. Focus on the reason you are at this point. Why did you leave the relationship? What about it did not work for you?

What have you learned and what characteristics will you look for in your next relationship? Make a list of the characteristics of your perfect relationship. Then, shred it or recycle it; let the list go energetically, so more positive traits can be added by the Universe, and trust that the perfect relationship is now coming to you. This will help you focus on what you are ready to experience in your next relationship instead of what you did not like in your last relationship.

Mourning is really important for the person being left, the person that actually feels hopeless, not the person doing the leaving. The person leaving starts to mourn the relationship way before they leave it. The person being left will have more processing to do to catch up to where the person who is leaving the relationship is at energetically. You may have moments of mourning if you are the one doing the leaving, but in those moments you choose how to respond and how to be. If you feel sad, then do some letting go and move forward. If you continue to be sad and do not do any letting go, then being sad has become a choice. How does that help you to be sad? What does this change for you or does it keep you trapped? Instead, focus on what will make you happy and what you would like to create in your life going forward. What are you creating in this moment and how is it helping you do what you are here to do? Always, look at the big picture and be objective to pull yourself out of a bad place, energetically.

## Become Aware of Your Triggers

You probably have anger, resentment, and frustration toward the person with whom you are ending the relationship. Make sure to notice what triggers you and when, so you can let that go. Let go of the issues the relationship had and the baggage that went along with it. Free yourself, because that is who you are hurting. Everything happens for a reason. This relationship is ending now because it was supposed to. You both got what you were supposed to from it and now it is no longer supporting either of you.

There are things that may trigger you. For example, if the other person is doing good or well without you. Remember, if the other person is able to move on and succeed in their life, energetically you do too. It does not matter if you helped get them to that point, because you no longer want to be with them. Instead of focusing on them and their future, focus on your future and purpose. Be happy that they no longer need you so you can be free to focus on things that make your being happy. Change routines and things that are continual reminders so you can move forward without constantly looking backwards.

Do not torture yourself. If you have items to divide, instead of thinking about the future holidays, upcoming events, or events you did together, remind yourself why this relationship is over. Why are you done with this relationship? Why did this relationship not work anymore? Did it ever really work? Instead of staying stuck and miserable, what can you do to move forward? Focus on new activities, passions, and hobbies.

Remember, you are not alone. You have other people in your life that you can go see that movie with or go to that event with. You probably already know where you are going to spend the holidays. There will be new people you can do those fun things with. People you enjoy being around. It does not have to be this sad reminder of the good memories from the past, rather focus on making new, happier memories because you are not happy to do these things with this person now. It can be an exciting time of new and different experiences that are good and happy. If it is not, do not do them!

## Moving Forward

Once you make the decision to leave the relationship because it feels right, it is important to stick to it, and move forward. For you and everyone else involved. Sending mixed signals can give false hope to the other person and cause confusion, and in the end make it harder on you. It is not fair for anyone involved. If necessary, revisit the reasons you made this decision in the first place. Again, focus on what your happy future will look like. If the other person keeps pulling on you energetically, or trying to engage you, then make sure you take a break from each other until you are both in a better place where you can let the other person be free.

"I am free. I let go of the past hurts from this relationship." Let them go and refill those spaces in you with: "I am free." "I am free to be happy and purposeful. My focus is_____." It is important to feel and let go, but to also think big picture. Yes, something is ending, but something is beginning. All the bad is not going to be a part of your daily life anymore. It will be something new and light, something that you are creating with purpose, hope, and love. The next chapter will help you energetically let go of any anger, frustration, and baggage so you can refill your core with your true state of being. Love and light.

# 7 – Exercises to Help You Move Forward

This chapter goes over the basic tools from my previous books to help you energetically get back in balance. These basics will help you in any moment of your life, but you will find them essential when you are experiencing problems in your relationships.

Sometimes, you will do all these exercises back-to-back, and sometimes you may only do one or two of them. Always, do what works for you and supports you most in that moment. If you find yourself getting stuck or not able to do an exercise, the exercises are explained in more depth in the first book, "In Light & Love: My Guide to Balance." Bringing in White Light, letting go, and using "I am" statements will help you move forward.

## *Finding Balance with White Light*

You are a being of love. Visually, this is seen as a White Light that shines through and around you. We are all made of White Light and we are all connected by it as well.

White Light is God, Love, the Universe, Source, or whatever you would like to call it. It is non-denominational, it just simply is. Before we inhabit our bodies, love is all we know. This is our truth and you can return to it in every moment.

White Light is everywhere. You will see the beams of White Light breaking through clouds and trees most often in nature. It is also shown in pictures of religious and spiritual people as a light surrounding them. White Light flows through you at all times. Imagine visually, that you are surrounded by it in a huge spotlight or beam of light and it flows gently like a stream through your being. By bringing it through your body, you are remembering that you are love and light, and that all is well.

When you feel out of balance, one thing you can do to get back into balance immediately is to bring White Light through your body. This will instantly balance your being (your body, mind, and spirit), and you will instantly feel calm and peaceful. White Light feels nurturing and supportive because it is. It helps you remember who you really are, a being of love. White Light grounds you and centers you.

If there is a problem in a relationship, it is very powerful and helpful energetically to put both of you in the White Light. They may not take it individually, but what you give to the relationship will come back to the relationship. White Light always calms charged and intense situations. Use it often, because it will help calm, balance, and nurture whatever you send it to.

## White Light Exercise

Use the White Light to return to your natural state of being and to create a safe space at any time. You will feel calm and peaceful. Always do the White Light before any energy work.

*Tips:* You can sit or stand; be comfortable. If you lay down, you may fall asleep. Do not cross your arms, legs, or any body parts as this will make it more difficult for the energy to flow freely, especially when you first begin practicing this.

*Visualization:* Close your eyes. Begin by bringing White Light through your body. Imagine the light beams you see that break through the clouds or shine through the trees. This is your visual to imagine. The White Light is nurturing and supportive.

*White Light:* Imagine the White Light shining down on you, through you, and around you. The White Light comes in through the top of your crown (top of your head), down your face, your neck, into your shoulders, down your chest and back, into your stomach, into your hips, down into your thighs, to your knees, down your legs, and into your feet. The White Light flows from the center of your feet, down into the Earth. You become one with the light and the light flows into you and into the Earth like a gentle stream.

You will feel calm, centered, and at peace. You will be grounded (this is why you bring the light through your feet and into the Earth.) The White Light flows through you like a continual stream and it looks as if it is a beam of light flowing through you. The White Light surrounds your whole being.

You can also give White Light to a situation or a person. Just let the White Light flow down onto them. Do not try to control them, what they feel, or the situation. Simply give them the light.

Open your eyes when you are ready.

## *Letting Go*

You can visualize White Light and feel the peace it provides you, but sometimes it is time to energetically clean out your being, especially after a fight or when there is a problem. For example, White Light fills you with love, but if you are already full of negativity, irritation, frustration, or really anything that is not of love, you just keep battling the darkness with the White Light. End this energetic battle by cleaning out all this junk that is holding onto the darkness.

You will know when you have letting go to do, just pay attention to how you feel emotionally, what you are thinking, and how your body feels. Letting go does not mean that you forget the experience or what you learned, it means you let go of the baggage from that experience. You will feel so much better after you let go, and you will be in a better place for whatever is happening in your life at that moment.

Some things for you to let go of in your relationship: feeling sad, guilty, hurt, angry, betrayed, lonely, or afraid that you will recreate this relationship with someone else. These are big things, but it is important for you to let them go so that things can shift and really happen in the best way for everyone.

Whatever you hold onto from this relationship, you will have to let go of at some point, or it will continue to reincarnate. It is best to heal as much as you can, when you can.

There are many different ways to let go whether it is through exercise, creating art, journaling, visualizing, etc.; the list goes on! Here is an exercise where you visualize the tension, stress, frustration, anger, sadness, etc., leaving your body.

## Letting Go Exercise

Letting go helps you release anything that is blocking you so you can be energetically free of the baggage. Holding onto it does not help you, it is an energetic weight that holds you back. Learn from it and let it go! Free your energy.

*White Light:* Bring the White Light through the crown of your head, into your feet, and into the Earth. It is a steady stream and you feel safe, comfortable, and at peace.

*Letting go:* Begin by noticing where there is darkness, tension, or gray smoke in your body. Start with the area that is calling your attention the most or where the White Light got stuck going through your body. Then, imagine sending that energy up into the sky or the Universe. The Universe is all love. The Universe will turn the energy into love and it will shrink into a speck of pepper before it disappears completely.

You can imagine pulling the energy out like a weed, you can stomp it out, or imagine it flowing out of your body like smoke. Whatever you see and feels right in that moment, do.

*White Light:* Bring the White Light through again and say your truths, "I am love. I am light. I am safe. I am whole. I am free. All is well." You can say this as often as you would like. If you resist one of these "I am" statements, check in with yourself and see what letting go you have to do around that statement.

*Tips for your body:* Sometimes, it helps to wiggle or shake that body part or move your body around if you are having a hard time moving the energy out of your body.

Water is always helpful as well if you are having a hard time moving energy. You may feel a pull to put your feet in water (whether a tub, bowl, pool, lake, stream, or even take a shower).

Sometimes, it is helpful to imagine a pastel color coming in from behind your body, pushing out the energy you are releasing, and filling all the spaces within you in that color. Use whatever pastel color comes to you and it may change while you are letting go as your energy shifts.

*Tips for your mind:* If you find your mind is holding onto an experience and the details, shift your focus. Instead, be grateful for that experience as you are letting it go. Everything happens for a reason. Why did this happen and what did you learn from experiencing it? For example, "In this experience I learned

_____. I am grateful for _____." Thank the Universe for the experiences you have had, especially the ones that seemed harder and really forced you to grow.

*Balance yourself:* When it feels like the tension, stress, energy, or whatever you were letting go of is less; bring the White Light through your body again. "I am _____."

*Check in:* Does it feel gone?

If it feels gone, go to next step, "More letting go."

If not, keep going for as long as you can. Remember to stay in balance with your body. If you are feeling that your body has done all it can right now, do more another day. Sometimes, you can let go of stuff right away and sometimes it takes more than one letting go session.

*More letting go:* Is there more letting go to do somewhere else in your body at this time? If you answer yes, release that energy if you can at this moment.

*Closing:* When you are finished, bring the White Light through your body, into your feet, and into the Earth.

Nurture and support your body the rest of the day, especially if you did a lot of letting go. A nap or early bedtime will help you renew and reset your body after a lot of letting go.

## Letting Go Tips

Letting go is like an onion. There are many layers and some may make you cry more than others. Energy moves quickly. Sometimes, you will find the energy is gone quickly and you do not even know what you let go of. Others may take a little bit more time and feel like they have more layers. Remember that anything not of love is an illusion and you can let it go as easily as you let it into your life. Do not try to remember what you let go of, simply let it go.

Only do as much as you can in one day. Stay in balance and pamper yourself, especially after an intense letting go session. Make sure that if you do a lot of letting go in one session that you have time for a nap or rest time afterwards. When you are letting go it may not feel like you are doing a lot, but you may be physically exhausted later.

Everything is connected not only in this life experience, but in others as well. Do not be surprised if you find yourself seeing or knowing of experiences that are from another life. If you are seeing something while you are letting go and you are getting to let go of it, do not question it. Just do it, especially if it connects with the relationship that just ended. Your mind cannot make this stuff up. Trust what you are seeing or feeling and then let it go.

Always make sure you bring the White Light through your body after you finish doing your letting go. This will help balance your being which is necessary after any energy shift you do.

## *"I am" Statements*

Words literally mean what they say and that is what you create in your life. Now that you are aware of their power, be aware of what you are creating. If you say you "want" something, you will want it and not get it. The same is true with words like need, want, desire, crave, etc. How often are you using these words? Notice what happens the next time you use them, you will find that you keep needing, wanting, desiring, and not actually receiving what you "want" especially in your relationships.

Use words that help you feel safe, connected, and at peace. What works for you today, may be different tomorrow. "I am" is the most powerful thing you say to the Universe. You can feel the power of these statements flow through your body the moment you think or say them.

"I am" statements that resonate with you will vary depending on what you are experiencing. However, there are some that are always true like: "I am love." "I am light." "I am safe." "I am whole." "I am free." These statements are always true and you can use them at any time.

Sometimes, you will decide to start off your day with an "I am" that will help you with whatever you are working on in your relationship. If you are having relationship problems, you may really connect with, "I am free." "I am love." "I am safe." "All is well." Do you connect with any of these right now? If so, use them throughout the day.

## "I am" Exercise

"I am" is a powerful statement that you can use to help support you regardless of what is happening around you. It helps you tell your mind what to focus on and it supports your being.

*White Light:* Bring the White Light through the crown of your head, into your feet, and into the Earth. It is a steady stream and you feel safe, comfortable, and at peace.

*"I am" statement:* Say your "I am" statement(s) and let the energy of the words flow through your body, just like the White Light. Imagine the words flowing from the crown of your head, into your feet, and into the Earth.

Open your eyes when you are ready.

## "I am" and Letting Go

"I am" statements are very nurturing and supportive to your body after you have done letting go in that area. These statements support your body and help reprogram that area. An area that was holding onto negativity gets cleared in the letting go session and is now reprogramming into the "I am" statement you are putting there.

While you are letting go say, "I am love. I am light. I am safe. I am whole." Always say these truths when you are letting go and let them flow through your body. They will empower you and help you with whatever you are releasing.

Feel free to say them in the order that supports you the most in the moment. If you are using one of these "I am" statements while you are letting go and you feel yourself rejecting it, you have some letting go to do around that "I am" statement. Once you do the letting go, the statement will help you feel more peace and calm.

Then you may use different "I am" statements in different parts of your body. Typically, the statement is an opposite statement of what you just released. For example, you may say, "I am free," in your lower stomach where you felt trapped. In your throat you may say, "I am speaking my truth." If you feel abandoned you may connect with, "I am supported." If you feel stuck say, "I am flowing." The shorter the "I am" statement, the easier it is to use.

After letting go each area may have a different "I am" statement or you may just use one for your whole being. Use whatever "I am" statement(s) that will support you in this moment. Make sure it is short and there are no negatives in the statement like, "I am not holding onto this negative energy any longer." Instead you could say, "I am free. I am whole."

Continue to use your letting go "I am" statements for at least three days after you do your letting go or until you find another "I am" that is more supportive to you. Every time you do letting go, see what other "I am" statements will support you with whatever you just let go of and use them with, "I am love. I am light. I am safe. I am whole. I am free."

# 8 – Creating Peaceful Relationships

Creating peaceful relationships begins within you. If you do not feel peaceful at your core, you will not be interested in participating in or creating peaceful relationships. What you feel within yourself is what you reflect in your life and attract to you.

Are you ready to consciously create peaceful relationships in your life? Not relationships that are fear-based or worry-based, rather relationships that are built on love, harmony, trust, acceptance, and peace. Are you ready to show compassion and tolerance for others, as well as, for yourself? What you create in your life does affect the world around you, so pay attention to what you are creating energetically and physically. Choose peace.

## *Honor Yourself*

When you honor yourself, it gives off an amazing energy vibration to everything on this planet and beyond. Pay attention to your intuition, listen to your instincts, follow your gut, and let yourself be guided onto a path that is fulfilling and purposeful for you. As you become whole with yourself, you become whole in all your relationships as well. Be true to yourself and you will notice how much freer, happier, and fulfilled you will be.

What other people say and do should not determine if you are happy in a relationship or not, because they are not you.

They do not have your lessons, experiences, and karma. You know what makes you happy and what makes you run in the other direction. Pay attention to what you already know and listen to how you feel. Follow your passions and anything that energizes you. By doing this, you honor yourself.

## Honor Yourself in Your Relationships

The best energy practice is to live your life in the best way possible not only for you, but for those around you as well. Begin by taking ownership for your role in the relationships in your life. You know if you have a connection with someone or if you are just stringing them along. The moment you know you are not happy in a relationship, it is time for you to do something about it. If you do not like how you feel around someone, then it is time to stop being around them as much as possible or completely. Perhaps, this involves talking to the other person so they are aware and can make a change, maybe it is drawing boundaries, or it is time to leave that relationship. Just know, the moment that you stay in any relationship you do not want to be in, the harder it gets for you to stay, and the more miserable you become because it is not right for you anymore. Honor yourself and listen to how your relationships are supporting you or how they are not anymore. You are always guided, listen to it.

When you find people you enjoy being with, spend time with them in a balanced way. Distance does make the heart grow fonder. If you find that you spend too much time with any one person, little things will start to bother you. It is best to balance the time you spend with everyone that way it is almost always a good experience. You know to eat certain foods in moderation, now start spending time around the people in your life in moderation too.

Pay attention energetically to the new people you bring into your life. You may not have been aware of why you were attracted to certain people before, but now that you are more energetically aware of relationships, you should be more aware of who you are allowing into your life. If you keep attracting the same people and it keeps ending the same way, you have letting go to do and a pattern to change. The goal is not to just surround yourself with a certain type of person or people to fill a void, rather to surround yourself with a base of people that are nurturing and supportive.

If you find that you have a void in your life and you are using people to help you with that emptiness, know that no one can fill that void for you. You have to let that void go, get to the core of why it is there, how it has supported you, and reconnect with the White Light. Find activities to do with friends and alone that stimulate you, make you feel happy and purposeful, and that you look forward to doing. Also, make sure you are connecting with the White Light throughout the day when you start to feel alone. This will energetically remind you that you are not alone and this void is an illusion. By letting go of any emptiness you feel within, you honor yourself by freeing your energy. Energetically, you are free; remember that in all of your interactions.

## Take Time to Be

Taking time to be is a very important way to honor yourself. It is important that you spend time quietly and you are still and silent. This can be done by meditating, being in nature hiking or sitting, or just relax and let your mind wander about nothing in particular. When you are alone and you give your intuition an outlet to update you, empower you, energize you, and guide you, you are being, instead of always doing. It gives you a chance to reflect on your life and for you to get some important insights that you may otherwise be too busy to notice.

Taking time to be can seem like one of the hardest things to do when you are always on the go. However, if you do not take time to be, you miss important clues, insights, and moments of clarity to help guide you along your path. It is always easier to schedule in time to be, instead of something happening to literally force you to be.

If you do not slow down and take care of yourself, illness or injuries may come into your life to help you do just that. Sometimes, there are signs to notice beforehand if you pay attention. You may think you are going to get sick, get in an accident, or get injured and then it happens. This is not attraction, rather your intuition trying to give you a warning, so pay attention. When you feel like you are doing too much or you are going to get sick, notice that you usually do. Honor your body by slowing down, spending time alone, and taking time to just be. It will recharge, reconnect, and realign your whole being.

## *Be Conscious*

Living consciously is bringing all the parts of this book together and using it in every moment. Take responsibility for your choices and experiences. Everyone is on their own journey and every journey is different. We are here to have our experiences, but in the end, we all return to a place of being one. Separation is an illusion. In that place of oneness, we are love, peace, and calm.

You choose the people you surround yourself with, so choose wisely. Notice the energy you are giving off to others and the energy you receive from them. Be aware of who you are attracting into your life and why. Your relationships should feel balanced and make you both happy. Do not hand your power over to others or ask others to hand their power over to you. We are all equals because we are all one. The next time you get mad at someone, remember that you are the exact same energy as them. What would be more helpful for both of you?

Treat others how you would like to be treated. Most people would like to be respected and cherished. If you cannot do those things for them, then set them free to people that can. This will also free your energy so you can use it in more fulfilling ways. Focus on your journey, connecting with your purpose, and how you can help spread more peace and love to everything on the planet. Do not worry about other people and their journey, that is their work. You can be there to support them, but you cannot do the work for them.

Be compassionate, honest, and trustworthy. The more purposeful and aware you are in your thoughts, words, and actions, the more you will flow through life. There will still be hiccups. Those always have a purpose and you have asked for them to be there but, you will create less problems for yourself when you act from a place of awareness. No matter what is happening in your life, remember there is a purpose. At all times you can only see a slice of the pie. The best thing to do is to follow your intuition, think big picture, and trust that everything works out in the best way possible for everyone involved, always.

## *Allow Abundance*

Abundance is so much more than money. Abundance is everything in your life from the people and opportunities in your life, to your experiences. If you believe you do not deserve nurturing, supportive people in your life, you will not attract them. On the flipside, if you believe you should have them in your life, you will attract them to you. Your thoughts about your home, work, and relationships do the same thing. If they are negative they push things away and if they are positive they attract them to you. Pay attention to your thoughts, your words, and your beliefs because that is what you are allowing into your life.

Begin by thinking big. Most people think small, are stuck in the past, and are afraid of something, usually failure. Chances are that you have forgotten how powerful you are and that miracles happen in your life to help you every day. You just have to notice them and be grateful for them to keep bringing in even more.

You often get sidetracked and forget your purpose. You stop doing the things you are passionate about. Instead, you focus on the things that stifle and prevent you from flowing through your life. Now it is time to remember what you are passionate about and to do things that make you truly happy. When you do this, you will start attracting more abundance into your life.

Remember that you are part of something bigger. Your thoughts, your words, and your actions impact more than just you. They create your reality and the reality around you. This affects others greatly.

## Physical Abundance

Physical abundance comes in many forms such as money, health, food, and the people in your life. Basically, it is anything that you can physically touch. Notice how all these pieces of physical abundance are playing out in your life. What is working and what is off balance? Are they all off balance? Are you paying attention to what your body is telling you? Remember, everything works out better when you are in a balanced place.

### *Money*

Being abundant is usually associated with how much money and wealth you have. While this is an important form of abundance in our culture, it is only one aspect that requires your awareness. Money has not always been the most important way to show abundance and it is already shifting from being the most important way. Through the centuries, money has meant different things, which means it shifts with society's beliefs, expectations, and goals.

What are your beliefs about your finances, how much money you should have, and what type of life you should be living? Does your childhood still heavily influence this? Are you letting yourself bring in whatever abundance is supposed to be coming into your life or what you think you should bring into your life? This is an important question, so please take a moment to actually think about this and respond. This tells you what you are financially allowing in your life and what is guiding your finances.

You are as abundant as you allow yourself to be. How do you think of money, spend it, and treat it? Money is energy just like everything else. Pay attention to what you are allowing into your life and creating with it. Being abundant is different for each person so you should not compare your abundance to anyone else. Your journey is different, you are here to experience different things, and money means different things to different people. Some people choose to have lots of things, others may prefer to have more experiences, and some like to be in the middle. Really, it is whatever you choose and what makes you happy, because that is what you create in your life. There is no right or wrong, you do not have to keep up with your family, friends, and neighbors. You just have to do what is right for you.

## Health

Health is often based upon your financial abundance. If you are worried and stressed all the time, that physically takes a toll on your body. Also, if you do not have money to eat or to eat food that is good for your body that can significantly impact your health.

Usually, issues with your health are based upon something you set into place before you were born, such as genetic health problems, illnesses, or life-threatening diseases. Remember, at some level, you create everything in your life and this includes health problems. Everything has a purpose. Illness and injuries often appear to get you back on track. Depending on why a health issue is happening determines on how quickly you recover from it or if you do not. Something bigger is always going on. Sometimes, you will know the reason when it is happening, and sometimes, you will find out much later. What are you creating and why?

## *Food*

Food is also a form of abundance, so enjoy what you are eating. Eat foods that support your body and food that your body appreciates. If you judge and feel bad about what you are eating, you literally are eating that negative energy. Remember, everything is best in moderation. If you think this food is a treat and you put positive energy into it, your body will process it better. Of course, if you continue to eat foods your body does not want you may have indigestion, stomach aches, or other problems.

What you think about your food as you eat it is an important part of the digestive process, so what are you thinking? If you are angry or upset, that is not the best time to eat. Do some letting go first, then enjoy a meal to replenish your body. Always, prepare and eat your food in a place of light and love.

## *The People in Your Life*

Another form of physical abundance is the people in your life. Do you surround yourself with positive people or negative people? The people in your life reflect you. If you do not like the people in your life, take a look at what you are doing, why, and how you treat yourself and others.

Allow abundance to flow into your relationships. Stop limiting yourself. Take a look at the patterns you have learned from your childhood and notice how they limit you. Abundance should flow into you and around you. When you find that you are limiting yourself, stop and then allow yourself to feel the abundance flowing into you. Allow abundant experiences, opportunities, love, happiness, and peace into your relationships. You are an abundant being. Let this truth flow into all of your relationships. Be free.

## Unseen Abundance

Unseen abundance is the energy that is going on behind the scenes that you cannot physically touch. Examples of unseen abundance are: spiritual abundance, emotional abundance, and your experiences.

## *Spiritual Abundance*

Spiritual abundance is knowing that you are never alone. You are always guided, supported, and love. Notice the word "love," and not "loved." While you are loved, that is external and comes from others. Love comes from within, from God, Universe, Source, or whatever term you prefer. You are that love and you have the ability to share that love with everything.

Your spiritual abundance is what helps you pull through your darkest hours. External things cannot help you, nor do they make you feel better when you have hit a rough patch. If you feel alone and that you have no spiritual abundance, depression will usually set in, and sometimes it, can be extremely difficult to shift or stop. Remember, what you put out comes back to you. If you feel alone, you will keep attracting experiences where you feel alone. If you feel nurtured, supported, and appreciated you will attract more of those experiences to you. Pay attention to what you are giving off and if you do not like it, change it. Every moment you can begin anew. The power is literally in this moment. Not the past and not in the future. What you do right now in this moment is what shapes your future.

*Emotional Abundance*

Emotional abundance is when you feel supported by yourself and possibly by others as well. When you feel happy, notice that you feel good, and you attract others in a good place to you as well. You also are not as affected by people that are angry or not in a good place. Usually, only when you are upset, angry, or not in a good place can the people around you easily take your unhappiness to a more intense level of unhappiness.

Allow yourself to feel what you are feeling, and if you find you do not want to feel that way anymore then, what can you do to change it? It may feel like your emotions get control over you, but really you control your emotions all the time. They only have a perceived control over you when they get ignored and pushed down for too long. Then, something else comes along and sets you off because you can no longer ignore them. Acknowledge your emotions and deal with the things that are coming to the surface in your life. Your emotions are also creating your next moment. What are you creating?

### *Your Experiences*

Your experiences are another form of abundance. If you truly appreciate the experiences that bring you joy, you will attract more of them to you. Whenever you are thankful for something, you bring more of that to you. If you enjoy the people you are with and the things you are doing, make sure to let them know. On the flipside, if you do not like the experiences in your life right now, what can you do so that you do enjoy them?

You will take your experiences with you from this life and into your other-life experiences. All of them and the baggage too, if you do not let it go. Remember, you are the creator in your life. You are a part of something bigger. How are you creating your life in a bigger, more purposeful, and more meaningful way? These are the experiences you will be eager to take with you into other-life experiences, so make more of them.

## *Be Free*

One of the phrases that people are enjoying most in their life right now is, "I am free." You are free until your expectations, fears, and beliefs limit you from doing what you would like to do. Stop limiting yourself. Of course, being free does not mean go out and hurt others or other things on the planet. That karma will not make you feel free. It means you are free to do the things that make you happy and that also lift up the people and energy of the Earth.

Surround yourself with people, experiences, and opportunities where you can be free. No one wants to be stifled or trapped, so do not put yourself in those situations anymore. If you are in a situation like that now, how can you free yourself? What would make you happy and free? Does the answer change if you only ask yourself what would make you free?

As a society, we think that there is a limit to our happiness, the other shoe is going to drop, and bad things are just a part of your life. Almost all movies and shows that we watch to entertain us, tell us this is the way things have to be, because if we just watch people being happy it gets boring; there has to be conflict and drama. Then, we create what we watch in fantasy worlds into our lives just to find out that it makes things worse. The reality is that you can be happy and free at the same time. The question is not if it is possible, rather the question is would you like to be happy and free? If so, what can you do to make this your reality?

It may take time to find what makes you happy and free, or you may know exactly what you have to do right now because you have been thinking about it. You can take baby steps if that is what it requires, or you can make a switch over night if that is possible. When you start to believe and truly know that you are free and happy, things will start to shift for you in ways you could not have imagined. Something or someone may try and keep you from staying in this place and when that happens, let it go and say, "I am free." "I am happy."

The time is now to release whatever is holding you back and keeping you from moving forward. You are not meant to be stagnant, miserable, or unhappy anymore. Any changes in your relationships that are happening are happening to help you move forward. Instead of fighting them, acknowledge that they are happening to you at this time for a purpose. You may not understand why, but things are changing to help you with something. Let the change help you move forward and remember; you are always free and happy. It is a choice, so choose it in your life. Be free!

# About the Author

Lisa is the author of "In Light & Love: My Guide to Balance," and "Energy Balance: My Guide to Transformation." She has been working as an Intuitive Energy Coach since 2002 and writes these books to help her clients and others get back into balance. Lisa was born with her intuitive abilities with energy healing and is a Reiki Master.

She has the ability to see, sense, hear, and feel energy. Lisa intuitively knows why, where, and how each person stores energy within their body, how to release that energy, and how to reprogram that area with positive energy.

Lisa currently lives in San Diego, California with her family. For more information about Lisa, her videos, and her events, visit www.lisagornall.com.

Follow her on Facebook at facebook.com/lisamgornall, Twitter @LisaMGornall, and on Instagram at energycoachlisa.

Made in United States
North Haven, CT
20 October 2021